THE UNIVERSITY OF
WINCHESTER

About this book

What future is there for the Left, faced with the challenges of the twenty-first century? Based on a lifetime's experience in politics, Marta Harnecker addresses the crisis facing the Left today.

At its heart, this book is a critique of social democratic realpolitik. Harnecker reminds us that, contrary to today's orthodoxy, politics is not the art of the possible but the art of making the impossible possible by building a social and political force capable of changing reality.

She believes that the social experiments being carried out in Latin America today hold out hope that an alternative to capitalism is possible; they are essentially socialist, democratic projects in which the people are the driving force. To create a real alternative to capitalism, though, the Left must change.

Rebuilding the Left offers real hope to those who still believe that we can create a different world.

D1145566

About the author

Sociologist, political scientist, journalist, activist, Marta Harnecker became one of the most widely read authors of the Latin American Marxist Left when *The Basic Concepts of Historical Materialism* was published at the end of the 1960s. There have been 63 editions and few books in the field of Marxist theory have sold as many copies.

After studying with Louis Althusser in Paris, Harnecker returned to her native Chile but had to go into exile in Cuba after the military coup against Salvador Allende's government. In Cuba, Marta Harnecker ran the research institute Memoria Popular Latinoamericana (Latin American Popular Memory (MEPLA)) and continued to write. To date, she has published over 60 titles. Her interest in the new political movements and their relationship to organic politics has been reflected in books such as *The Left after Seattle*, and her most recent publication, *The Left on the Threshold of the Twenty-First Century*. An ardent defender of the Bolivarian revolution, she has also published *Understanding the Venezuelan Revolution: Hugo Chávez talks to Marta Harnecker*; *Venezuela: militares junto al pueblo*; and *Venezuela: una revolución sui generis*.

Marta Harnecker

Rebuilding the Left

Translated by Janet Duckworth

Zed Books
LONDON AND NEW YORK

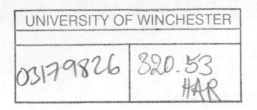
Rebuilding the Left was first published in 2007 by
Zed Books Ltd, 7 Cynthia Street, London N1 9JF, UK and
Room 400, 175 Fifth Avenue, New York, NY 10010, USA.

www.zedbooks.co.uk

Cover designed by Andrew Corbett
Set in 11/13 pt Perpetua by Long House, Cumbria, UK
Printed and bound in the EU by Biddles Ltd
www.biddles.co.uk

Distributed in the USA exclusively by Palgrave Macmillan, a division of
St Martin's Press, LLC, 175 Fifth Avenue, New York, NY 10010.

A catalogue record for this book
is available from the British Library

US Cataloging-in-Publication Data
is available from the Library of Congress

ISBN 978-1-84277-256-0 Hb
ISBN 978-1-84277-257-7 Pb

Contents

*To Michael Lebowitz, my partner,
with whom I share so many hopes and dreams
and to President Chávez for having renewed hope
in Our America and the world.*

Introduction

We live in a world that is nothing like the world of 50 years ago. Ours is a world characterised by the defeat of socialism in Eastern Europe and the Soviet Union and the transformation of the United States into the world's biggest military power with no countervailing force at all, a situation that has dealt a heavy blow to the Left and progressive forces. Ours is a world marked by the advances made by the scientific-technical revolution and their effect on the productive process and on nature: the globalisation of the economy and culture and the increasing power of the mass media. We live in a world where capitalism in its most brutal guise, neo-liberalism, uses technological advances for its own benefit and is wreaking havoc on much of the world's population and ruthlessly destroying nature as it creates 'not only rubbish that the environment cannot recycle but also human cast-offs who are difficult to recycle socially', pushing social groups and whole nations into collective neglect.[1]

A growing discontent, nevertheless, has begun to make itself felt among extended social sectors. This discomfort has begun to transform itself, first into passive resistance and then into active resistance. In the last few years – and in spite of the social fragmentation strategy applied by neo-liberalism to try and neutralise this resistance – it has begun to manifest itself openly in demonstrations and actions against the existing global system, thus giving rise to a new international cycle of struggles.

New horizons are opening up but the challenges we face are enormous. And we are not in the best shape to take them on. We need to rebuild the Left – and urgently. To do this we must first take a harsh look at the weaknesses, mistakes and deviations that hang heavily over our past and we must make sure that we know what caused them because that is the only way we will be able to overcome them. This book wants to make a contribution to that effort.

One of my central points is the criticism of the concept of politics as the art of the possible, for this leads us to adapt ourselves opportunistically to what exists. I argue that for revolutionaries politics is the art of making the impossible possible, not from some voluntarist urge to change things but because our efforts should be realistically focused on changing the current balance of power so that what appears to be impossible today becomes possible tomorrow.

Another very important point is the reflection on what kind of political instrument we need if we are to respond to the new challenges that the twenty-first century places before us: a tool that will allow us to build a social and political force that makes possible the profound social changes we are fighting for. If we are to achieve this objective we must overcome the organic forms of the past, which were the result of an acritical copying of the Bolshevik model of the party, and get rid of the theoretical underpinnings of this model. These underpinning do not take any account of one of Marx's central ideas: social practice as the action that allows men and women to transform themselves at the same time as they transform the circumstances that surround them, and in doing so achieve a higher level of human development.

In my opinion, however, criticising the organic form of party or organisation used in the past does not mean denying the need for a political instrument, as it does for some other theorists. I think such an instrument is essential because history has shown us that the construction of a popular anti-capitalist social force is not something that happens spontaneously: it needs a builder-subject that is able to use an analysis of the whole social and political dynamic to guide its actions; a subject capable of developing the political strategy that makes it possible to glue together the most diverse social and political sectors in opposition to existing neo-liberal globalisation, on an international as well as a national level; a political instrument that coordinates the action of the multiple, plural subject while respecting differences and determining what are the most appropriate tactics for breaking the power of the ruling classes and beginning to move towards building a society that turns its back on the perverse, individualistic logic of capital to begin to develop an increasingly humanistic and solidarity-based logic – a political instrument that allows us to begin to build a socialism for the twenty-first century whose final goal is fuller human development.

After dealing with all of these questions, I end by analysing the subject of reform and revolution and I show how these concepts apply to the Bolivarian revolutionary process, a *sui generis* revolutionary process that has forced the Latin American Left to rethink many things.

This book – which brings together many reflections and whole sections from work I published between 1999 and May 2006[2] – has been to a large extent inspired by the practice of the Latin American revolutionary movement itself. (I have been making a systematic record of this practice over the last fifteen years in a work of recovering historical memory).[3] I should warn the reader that I have not made an exhaustive study of the available bibliography; I have used mostly those books which I had at hand. However, the English-speaking reader may find that I refer to the work of several Latin American writers to whom they have not had previous access. If an important author's book is not among those that I have consulted, this is not because I deliberately left it out, but simply that, at the time of writing, I had not been able to study it with the attention it deserves.

I would have liked to have gone into many of the topics in greater depth and there are many others I haven't even touched on. I hope that my readers will understand the limitations of this book and will feel encouraged to go more widely and deeply into the subjects dealt with – many of which are, I know, polemical – and bring new points of view to bear on them. If I manage to achieve this, I will have met one of the goals I set myself – for I consider this to be an open book, and part of a collective effort.

I wish to thank Michael Lebowitz, my partner with whom I share so many hopes and dreams, for his valuable suggestions. I thank him for his patience in putting up with me in the midst of all the tension that arises when one tries to combine time for reflection with the myriad tasks that are set by concrete political practice.

I most especially wish to thank President Chávez for having renewed hope in Our America and the world.

I hope that this book does its little bit towards rebuilding the Left by contributing ideas which help to stimulate a new political culture in our ranks: a culture, as I have said on other occasions, that is pluralist and tolerant. A culture that leaves everything that divides us on the back burner and puts everything that unites us first. That unites us around values such as solidarity, humanism, respect for difference and the defence of nature. That turns its back on the desire for gain and the laws of the market as the chief motivators of human activity. That begins to awaken to the fact that being radical is not a matter of advancing the most radical slogans, or of carrying out the most radical actions – which only a few join in because they scare off most people. Being radical lies rather in creating spaces where broad sectors can come together and struggle. For as human beings we grow and transform ourselves in the struggle. Understanding that we are many and are fighting for the same objectives is what makes us strong and radicalises us. Revolutionary politics can only be conceived of as the art of making the impossible possible.

PART 1
The Left and the New World

Chapter 1
Profound Changes in the World

1   We live in a world very different from the one that existed half a century ago at the beginning of the Cuban Revolution, not only because of the defeat of Soviet socialism in the East – which was an extremely hard blow for the Left – but also because of the effect of other events. We will mention only the discoveries made by a new scientific-technological revolution and their effects on the productive process and nature; the mass media's increasingly important role; neo-liberalism's installation as the hegemonic system; and the role played by foreign debt in subjugating Third World economies to the interests of the great powers.

2   The machine tools that accelerated the development of industrial civilisation are being replaced rapidly by digitally controlled machine tools,[4] and robots and computers – which allow data and knowledge to be automatically compiled, processed and produced – are becoming essential in the workplace.

3   But it's not just computers: the *electronic information revolution* has caused fundamental changes in telecommunications, microbiology and other areas. Daily life in developed countries is swamped with information technology gadgets: credit cards, the electronic cards used as hotel keys, smart traffic lights, doors which open and close automatically and thousands of other things.

4   The new technologies make it easier to disseminate ever greater quantities of data and enormously increase the power of calculation while reducing its cost. This in turn means that scientific knowledge evolves at an extremely rapid rate.

5   An example of the growth of knowledge is the spectacular development in biotechnology and genetic engineering.

6   The power to use 'genetic information to create "new" organisms
and to put the forces that guide life's metabolism at the service of the
production of wealth is a technological leap that has unimaginable
consequences'.[5]

7   According to Jeremy Rifkin these technological-scientific developments
hold up a mirror to a world where crops grown in laboratories could be
harvested on a large scale. Nevertheless, some thought should to be given
to the consequences this could have for the hundreds of millions of people
who depend on agricultural work for their survival.[6] Moreover, trade,
finance, recreation, and research have been profoundly shaken by these
new technologies.

A unit in real time on a planetary scale

8   Capital today not only moves into the most remote parts of the world – as
it has been doing since the sixteenth century – but is capable of function-
ing, in real time and on a planetary scale, as a single unit. Vast quantities of
money – billions of dollars – are transferred in seconds by electronic
circuits which link the financial world. This is a phenomenon which only
became possible in the last few decades of the twentieth century thanks
to 'the new infrastructure brought into being by information and
communication technologies'[7] and by the new institutional order which
made these huge capital movements possible, once the barriers imposed
after the Second World War were removed.[8] This phenomenon developed
even more rapidly with the disintegration of the Soviet bloc and the
economic changes carried out by its former members. The world now
increasingly functions as a single operational unit, as a global capital
market.

The internationalisation of the production process

9   But over and above what is happening in the financial sphere there is
something qualitatively new happening in the field of production: the
internationalisation of the production process itself, with different parts
of the final product being manufactured in different geographical

locations.[9] And the same thing has occurred with many services. This displacement or relocation of the productive process and of services has meant that much production and many services have moved to the countries that offer more advantages, the most labour-intensive industries relocating to those countries in the South where labour is cheaper for many reasons, including state repression. And this, in its turn, has caused capitalist relations of production to propagate and to displace pre-capitalist relations in those places where transnational capital sets up shop.[10]

The transnational companies or global networks

10   The most powerful companies in the information age organise their operations on a world scale, and create what Robert Reich called the *global web or net*.[11] Finished products include components produced in many different parts of the world, which are then assembled using a new, more flexible and personalised form of production and marketing to meet the needs of specific markets.

11   Nations now trade not so much in finished products as in specialised forms of problem solving (problems of research, design, manufacture), specialised forms of problem identifying (marketing, advertising, client advisory services) and specialised forms of consulting services such as financial, research, legal and routine production services; all of these are combined to create value. That makes it very difficult these days to say which part of the product was made where.[12]

12   As Robert Reich[13] has argued, it is impossible to have vertical management structures and centralised ownership in today's highly profitable companies organised in networks. This, however, used to be the structure of US multinational companies: they had their head offices in the United States; their subsidiaries, located in other countries, really were subsidiaries, answerable to the interests of their head offices; and control and ownership were indisputably American. Power and wealth, rather than being concentrated in one country, have been dispersed into the hands of those groups that have obtained the now valuable skills of problem solving and problem identifying, and those groups can be found all over the world.[14]

13   With large-scale production you knew where a given product originated because it was made in a given place. The informational economy,

however, can produce efficiently in many different places: a computer may be designed in California, financed in the United States and Germany, and use memory cards made in South Korea; a jet plane designed in Washington and Japan may be assembled in Seattle from tail parts made in Canada, other parts from China and Italy, and an engine from the United Kingdom.[15] These are the reasons that lead Reich to talk of *transnational companies*.[16]

International trade: trade within large transnational firms

14 One result is that much of what we call international trade is actually trade within large transnational firms. For example, Stephen Poloz points out that a large percentage of US international trade takes place within multinational companies that are dealing abroad with themselves.

15 'Almost one-half of all American imports come from all-in-the-family foreign affiliates, and almost one-third of all American exports go to them. The share of US imports coming from intra-firm transactions: Mexico and Germany, 67 per cent; Japan, 77 per cent; Singapore, 74 per cent; South Korea, 56 per cent, a doubling in the past 10 years; China, 21 per cent, another doubling; Eastern Europe, 32 per cent – this is three times the previous figure.'[17]

16 It is important to understand, however, that we cannot identify multi-national firms with the US. Peter Drucker notes that 'American-based multinationals are only a fraction – and a diminishing one – of all multi-nationals. Only 185 of the world's 500 largest multinationals – fewer than 40 percent – are headquartered in the United States (the European Union has 126, Japan 108). And multinationals are growing much faster outside the United States, especially in Japan, Mexico and, lately, Brazil. The world economy of multinationals has become a truly global one, rather than one dominated by America and by US companies.'[18]

Change in the international balance of power

17 Drucker also points to the change in the international balance of forces. 'The new world economy is fundamentally different from that of the fifty years following World War II. The United States may well remain the political and military leader for decades to come. It is likely also to remain the world's richest and most productive national economy for a long time (though the European Union as a whole is both larger and

more productive). But the US economy is no longer the single dominant economy.'

18   'The emerging world economy is a pluralist one, with a substantial number of economic "blocs". Eventually there may be six or seven blocs, of which the US-dominated NAFTA is likely to be only one, coexisting and competing with the European Union (EU), MERCOSUR in Latin America, ASEAN in the Far East, and nation-states that are blocs by themselves, China and India. These blocs are neither "free trade" nor "protectionist", but both at the same time.' [19] In particular, we see the rapid growth of China and India at this time, both as recipients of investment by multinational firms and, increasingly, through the development of their own multinationals.

19   Finally, it should not be forgotten that what is being globalised today is nothing other than the capitalist form of exploitation. This takes on different forms according to a country's level of development. Whereas in the most developed countries the forward march of the technological revolution is obvious and has led some authors to think that we have already arrived at a post-industrial and even post-capitalist age, [20] in those countries where there is scant development huge numbers of workers have only recently joined the capitalist system of production.

20   One of the tasks we still have to undertake is to study the unequal way in which this process of exploitation takes place.

21   These technological changes revolutionise not only the production process but also all aspects of people's lives. For that reason some authors talk of a civilisational transformation. [21] They say this is not just another technological revolution [22] but something much deeper. Alvin Toffler, for example, claims that this is 'something as far-reaching as that first wave of changes unleashed ten thousand years ago by the appearance of agriculture or the second industrial revolution.' In his opinion, 'humanity is facing the biggest social upheaval and creative restructuring of all times'. [23]

22   Other authors, nevertheless, argue that no matter how important the current technological changes are, they cannot in any way be compared to the industrial revolution at the end of the eighteenth and beginning of the nineteenth century because the machines introduced into the production process at that time are still the 'technological foundation of contemporary production'. [24]

The nature of the state changes but its role is not reduced

23 These transnational companies try to free themselves from the clutches of the state in order to be able to operate without restrictions; they do, however, look to the governments of these countries to smooth the way for their business operations, converting ministries of foreign affairs and other government departments into veritable business offices serving their interests.[25]

24 It is fairly well known that 'active intervention by many governments has been decisive in stimulating their companies' competitiveness'.

25 Besides, Chomsky says that 'one of the best studies [it's from the 1990s] on the 100 biggest transnational companies on Fortune's list found that all of them had benefited from express intervention by their home governments.... We would not have many big corporations if it were not for public financing; and public financing comes from the taxpayer.'[26]

26 The blockade on Cuba is a good example of just how little independence transnational companies have from US government policy.

27 But nation states, even as they intervene to help transnational capital, are increasingly losing control over a series of matters, either because the countries in a given region integrate to form a larger regional unit, such as the European Union, or because of the subordinate character of the less developed countries vis-à-vis the developed world. In the latter case, economic policies tend to be decided outside their borders. As the international monetary market, the world media and the big multinational companies grow stronger, so national unions, parties and communications systems become weakened.[27]

28 'Too often in contemporary discussions about globalisation authors assume that this is an exclusive alternative: either nation-states are still important or there has been a globalisation of the figures of authority. We must understand instead', Hardt and Negri say, 'that both are true: nation-states remain important (some, of course, more than others), but they have nonetheless been changed radically in the global context.'[28]

29 Far from witnessing a global capitalism where the state is unrecognised, what we are seeing is a great level of differentiation between very active states, like the Group of Seven, and 'a group of highly politicised capitalist

classes which make a great effort to establish what Stephen Gill correctly called, "a new constitutionalism for a disciplinary neo-liberalism",[29] while the least developed countries go on getting weaker and weaker.

More limited democratic regimes

30 If we look at Latin America in particular, we can see that the democratic regimes existing today differ greatly from those existing before the era of the dictatorships. In those years, according to Carlos Ruiz, the level of social and economic development created an allegiance among the masses that was sufficiently broad-based to provide stability for bourgeois democratic representative regimes by incorporating certain popular sectors into political struggles. 'It was the era of the alliance between sectors of the working class, those fringes of the middle layers that had arisen under the aegis of the state and industrialists ... under a pattern of capitalist development in which industry became the driving force not only behind economic growth and capital accumulation but also behind the social and cultural organisation of society and the organisation of political struggle within the system's framework.'[30]

31 It was probably both the end of the long period of post-war expansion, the beginning of the new profound crisis which was gestating at this time and also the rise of the class struggles which jeopardised the existing system of domination and led to dictatorships being installed in several countries in Latin America (Brazil, Uruguay, Chile, Argentina). It was only possible to create the political conditions for the capitalist restructuring that was needed through force-based regimes which dismembered the popular classes and their social and political representatives.

32 And then, when the soldiers went back to their barracks and negotiated a democratic way out, it could only be a limited democratic way out that prevented any repetition of the situations of ungovernability which had given rise to the dictatorial governments.

33 As Franz Hinkelammert says, the result was an 'aggressive kind of democracy, lacking consensus, where the media is almost completely controlled by concentrated economic interests; where sovereignty lies not with civil governments but with the armies, and over and above them, with international financial organisations which represent the governments of [more developed] countries. These are controlled democracies where the controllers are not themselves subject to any democratic mechanism.'[31]

34   These tutelage, limited, restricted, controlled or low-intensity democratic regimes – as they are called by various authors – concentrate power in bodies of a permanent, non-elected nature. The latter are not affected by changes resulting from elections and include the Council for National Security, the Central Bank, economic advisory institutions, the Supreme Court, the Auditor General, the Constitutional Court, and other similar institutions which drastically limit democratically elected authorities' ability to act.

35   Today groups of professionals, not politicians, take the decisions or exert a decisive influence over them. In fact, in some essential areas such as the economy and the military, institutions arise that are more like national subsidiaries of a supranational body:[32] the IMF, NATO, the World Bank, the European Parliament, 'which, domestically, inside countries, are able to condition or impose important actions, paying no heed to the electorate's opinion'.[33]

36   The apparent neutrality and non-political nature of these bodies conceal the new way the ruling class 'does politics'. Their decisions are adopted outside the political parties. This, according to Martín Hernández, makes it possible, 'to a certain extent, to cover up the class nature of the state apparatus by portraying decisions as the affair of foreign experts who apply "scientific" criteria and have no interest in demagogy; above all, as the real importance of elected institutions decreases, it becomes possible to create mechanisms for inter-bourgeois conflict resolution in which the masses are not called on to participate'.[34]

37   In fact, bourgeois democracies have always sought to protect themselves from the decisions of the dominated. But, in previous democratic regimes, these protection mechanisms were portrayed as failures of democracy, that is, as anti-democratic procedures: for example, restrictions on the right to vote or election frauds. However, these procedures were necessary to ensure the election of people trusted by the ruling classes, precisely because state authorities elected by universal suffrage actually *had the ability to influence* the way the state apparatus functioned.[35]

38   According to Hernández, this provided arguments in support of a reformist strategy because, if progressive forces were elected, they actually could carry out important social and political transformations, 'given the real influence elected authorities had over the way the state apparatus functioned'. Where did the illusory nature of reformist strategy

lie? In the belief that the behaviour of the ruling classes would be consistent with their democratic discourse. But that is not what happened. Once the ruling classes lost control of the government, they wasted no time in having recourse to the backbone of the state apparatus, the armed forces – backed directly or indirectly by the Pentagon – to cancel out democracy and establish a dictatorship, as happened with Arbenz in Guatemala, Bosch in the Dominican Republic, Goulart in Brazil and Allende in Chile.

39   The current situation is different: democracy has been 'improved'[36] since it has now become more difficult to distort the will of the electorate at the polls thanks to more sophisticated control procedures which use new information technology (the scandalous electoral frauds of the past are not now commonly seen). However, this improvement goes hand in hand with drastic restrictions. On the one hand, the mechanisms for manufacturing consent which greatly affect the 'will' of the electorate and are monopolised by the ruling classes have been vastly improved and, on the other hand, democratically elected authorities' ability to get things done has been greatly restricted as a way of establishing some kind of protection against the will of the citizenry. At the same time as everything is done to make sure the people's will is respected at the ballot box, the sphere of action of that will is restricted by setting limits on what the people's elected representatives can do.

40   The way modern state apparatuses function greatly restricts a left government's ability to act. 'Little is achieved by electing rulers who embody the people's will if their field of action' is so restricted 'that they can only operate in the realm of the insubstantial'.[37]

41   To the foregoing we should add that, although in some countries, notably Chile, limited spaces for political democratisation at the top were created when the military returned to barracks there is no concomitant 'democratisation of the institutions at the base of society (schools, factories, town councils, universities, etcetera....'[38]

42   The form that this type of authoritarian democracy takes depends on the particular features of each country's political history. Restrictive democracy – as Helio Gallardo says – 'is the theoretical model for a tendency and does not exist in a pure form. It includes authoritarian regimes with electoral, constitutional and armed forces support ... constitutional party governments with a coalition-type electoral base and

military surveillance as in Chile.... There are also authoritarian party regimes where the rule of law is weak or non-existent, there is military and corporate backing and mass mobilisation or a client electorate, as in the Mexican case.'[39]

43   Although the Central American political regimes that emerged out of the political negotiations with guerrilla forces or after a revolutionary process like that of the Sandinistas can also be labelled restricted democratic regimes, they don't have the same characteristics as the rest of the countries in Latin America. In the Nicaraguan case, the government was handed over to Violeta Barrios de Chamorro within the legal framework developed by the revolution and it was only under enormous pressure from the United States that the Sandinista influence over the army and the police was counteracted. In El Salvador, the 1993 demilitarisation agreements placed both numerical and functional limits on the role of the armed forces.

44   From the 1980s on, another kind of state reform began to be implemented in Latin America: the territorial relocation or decentralisation of given aspects of the state apparatus. 'In essence, this consists in territorially reordering the urbanisation process and manufacturing and service location as well as in handing over some responsibility for education, health, social assistance, housing and local economic development to states, regions, provinces or local councils.'[40] This reform has both economic and political objectives. On the one hand, it aims to facilitate the development of capitalism and on the other to break the popular movement apart and to divert its attention from global struggles to local demands. Nevertheless, this decentralisation process has perhaps had the least success [of all these measures] in achieving its aims. In fact, the Latin American Left has made most progress in the last few years in the area of local government. It has not only won increasingly large local spaces but in the most exemplary cases has turned them into the perfect place for showing the public that it is possible to implement policies that offer an alternative to neo-liberalism, something that is very important at a time when paradigms are in crisis, as they are now. [41]

Demobilising democracy and an indebted citizenship

45   But this is not all; Tomás Moulián, in reference to the current situation in Chile, has said that such democracies are not only *tutelage democracies* but also *demobilising democracies*.[42]

46   This demobilisation of the people can be attributed to a series of factors no longer chiefly linked to the use of repression or to other methods of putting pressure on the popular movement.

47   The most important factors are the decline of the union movement – very much as a result of the limits imposed on it by labour legislation enacted under the military dictatorship but still in effect – and the flexibilisation introduced into labour relations. 'All of this creates a considerable increase in labour instability, leaves workers unprotected and gives the employers more power to control them. Strategies of [rewarding] individual merit appear as more productive than strategies of collective coordination.'[43] And all of this is made worse with the new organisational methods in companies which try to create an *esprit de corps* among the workers and a subjective identification with the result of their work.

48   Another element which helps promote governability is consumerism. The culture transmitted by the media is not a culture of community but one of individual hedonism. People assign more and more importance to the search for comfort and question the legitimisation of consumerism less and less, tendencies which the credit system encourages. People are not content to live within their means, but prefer to live in debt and therefore need to have a steady job – something that is harder and harder to find – in order to be able to meet their economic commitments.

49   At this point it is perhaps important to remember that the phenomenon of mass consumption is not something that arose spontaneously; nor, as Rifkin says, did it stem from insatiable human nature. On the contrary, several studies show that at the end of the nineteenth century US workers were content to earn enough to live on and buy a few little luxuries. They preferred to have more leisure time than more income earned by working longer hours.[44] We must remember that Middle American behaviour patterns were very much influenced by the Protestant work ethic whose key tenets were moderation and thriftiness.[45]

50   How then, given these circumstances, did consumerism come into being?

51   It was, according to Rifkin, the US business community which set out to *radically change the psychology that had built the nation*. In the 1920s, US manufacturers were faced with a situation of overproduction resulting from a huge increase in industrial productivity which went hand in hand

with a drop in the number of consumers – technical change had left a growing number of people unemployed. This dramatic drop in sales could only be met head on if the US people's psychology could be changed by persuading people to consume more goods. So a huge crusade was launched to turn US workers into a herd of consumers. 'Marketing, which had previously played a peripheral role in business affairs, took on a new importance.'[46] The country had to change from a producer culture to a consumer culture and in order to do that it was necessary to transform goods that had previously been luxuries for higher-income groups into needs for lower-income groups.

52 '... advertisers began to shift their sales pitches from utilitarian arguments and descriptive information to emotional appeals to status and social differentiation. The common man and woman were invited to emulate the rich... . "Fashion" became the watchword of the day as companies and industries sought to identify their products with the vogue and the chic.'[47]

53 Hire purchase sales also appeared at this time. 'In less than a decade, a nation of hardworking, frugal Americans were made over into a hedonistic culture in search of ever-new avenues of instant gratification.' At the end of the 1920s '60 percent of the radios, automobiles, and furniture sold in the United States were purchased on installment.'[48]

54 Great success was achieved on a mass level in making the superfluous a necessity; in doing so and in promoting credit sales, a new *mechanism of domestication* was created, as Tomás Moulián says.[49]

55 Indebtedness on a mass scale works not only to sustain or expand the domestic market but also as a device to foster social integration.[50] People need to ensure they have a job and do their work well in order to be promoted so they can keep on consuming: buy their own house, a car, the latest audio equipment, the latest model television.

56 'The current model, unlike the import substitution market model, does not rely on populist policies, it relies on condemning workers to the prison of their debt, slaves to the constant seduction of objects which are placed before their eyes as essential if they are to really live. What energy for participating, for mobilising, what capacity for risk-taking can workers have when they are faced with both job instability and with religiously paying their hire purchase instalments since failure to pay the

latter transforms them into sub-humans, people who are denied their dreams of future comfort.'[51]

57   Another demobilising factor has been the appearance of a neo-liberalised Left which has substituted a belief in democratic capitalism for a belief in socialism; a Left which simply does not question the system and which, when mass mobilisations appear, manages them according to *strict group interest logic.*

58   Moulián sums up his thesis in this way: 'historical experience demonstrates that neither a dictatorship nor even the existing form of a "tutelage democracy" is needed to maintain the neo-liberal model. What it does need is the discipline of a "demobilising democracy" with a weak workers' movement which make only self-interested, economistic demands, with a Left that helps to legitimise the system and with "masses" more interested in consuming and entertainment than in public affairs.'[52]

The communications revolution in the service of capital

59   But, if there is anything that has undergone a profound transformation with the technological revolution, then that thing is communications. These too have been thoroughly revolutionised. Not so long ago, sound, image and text were separate, the most that had been achieved was to superimpose one on the other, as in the 'talkies'. Today, with digital technologies, for the first time in human history these different forms of information – text, data, sound and images – can be combined in a single product, the famous 'multimedia',[53] and they can be broadcast almost instantaneously.

60   'The influence of multimedia is becoming a strategic subject in political, technological, industrial and cultural spheres. The appearance of new products (electric editing with CD-ROMs, educational software, microcomputers ... multimedia terminals) and new services (searching databases at work or at home, telework, Internet) depend on the fusion of information sciences, television, telephones and satellites through the ascendancy of digital technologies.'[54]

61   One of the areas where scientific-technical discoveries have had the greatest impact is the development of the mass media. Satellites, fibre

optics and cable TV systems have revolutionised communications and make it possible to break time and space barriers. *For the first time, history will unfold in a single time: world time.*[55]

62   These technological inventions mean that people separated by oceans and continents can speak to each other just by pushing a few buttons. They help to eliminate the city's cultural advantages over rural areas.[56]

63   Television has become a *machine for communicating.*[57] That has a tremendous impact because most of what it broadcasts is experienced by viewers as real. Critical distancing is very difficult. However, the reality shown by the media does not exist for the vast majority of viewers.

64   The small screen invades homes, taking up more and more of people's free time and subliminally inculcating a neo-liberal, individualist, conformist ideology. One of its most effective weapons is most soap operas which put the people's consciousness to sleep and turn them into [soap opera] addicts. *They are the opiate of the people in today's world.*[58]

Cultural homogenisation

65   According to Eduardo Galeano the world has never been so unequal from an economic standpoint and yet, on the other hand, there has never been such a levelling off of things connected to ideas and morality. There is an obligatory uniformity hostile to the planet's cultural diversity. And there is not even any way to measure this cultural levelling. The electronic age's media, which serve a lack of human communication, are forcing unanimous worship of neo-liberal society's values down our throats.[59]

66   A sterile uniformity is spreading over everything. From one end of the earth to the other the same lifestyle, advocated by the mass media, is being imposed on everyone. 'People everywhere watch the same films, the same television serials, the same news, listen to the same songs, the same advertising jingles, wear the same clothes, drive the same cars, are surrounded by the same urbanism, the same architecture, the same kind of apartments, often furnished and decorated in an identical style.... In the wealthy districts of the world's big cities, the charm of diversity yields to the devastating offensive of standardisation, homogenisation, and uniformity.' Everywhere global culture reigns triumphant.[60]

67   Many authors think that what has been called cultural globalisation is

nothing other than 'the Americanisation of culture all over the world'.[61] Universal American culture, which some call McWorld, seems irresistible. In Japan, for example, hamburgers and chips have replaced noodles and sushi; to seem 'cool', young people use half-understood English expressions when they quarrel. In France, where less than ten years ago cultural purists waged war on that abomination Franglais, economic health is measured by the success of Disneyland-Paris. The sudden appearance of Halloween as a new French holiday simply to give a boost to business in the slow period before Christmas is merely the most disturbing example of this tendency to Americanise.[62]

68   The two hundred thousand million dollars the United States spends on advertising is money well spent. In order to create a worldwide demand for US goods, the need to consume them world-wide must also be manufactured and to do that the big companies like Coca-Cola cannot limit themselves to adverts about their product. They also have to extol the 'American way' at the same time.[63]

69   Marcuse's old reflections about the distinction between true and false needs have lost none of their relevance![64]

70   And since this culture creates the same need to consume both in those who have the means to satisfy that need and in those who don't – we must remember that one thousand million people on this earth live in extreme poverty – why should we be amazed when crime increases in step with consumerism, given that the same media which advertise all these products also broadcast detailed information on how to acquire them illicitly via the films they broadcast to millions?

71   What really moulds the way people think, with all the danger that implies, are the powerful audiovisual instruments. Their ownership is increasingly concentrated in fewer hands, dominated by big trans-nationals who manipulate information to serve the interests of the ruling classes.[65]

The need for intellectual self-defence

72   The media's power of thought control and manipulation is so great that, in Noam Chomsky's opinion, people need to take a course in intellectual self-defence to protect themselves from their effects.[66]

73   I think it is tragic to see how indifferent the Latin American Left and

many of the continent's intellectuals are towards this cultural colonisation. It is symptomatic that people seem to think it natural and even try to justify the fact that more and more English words appear on billboards, in notices and in books in our countries.

74   I think it is strategically necessary for those fighting for a different kind of society to know when and how to build a restraining wall against this type of penetration. And in that sense, it seems obvious to me that in this era of globalisation and the Internet, this wall cannot be outside our consciousness. I think that to talk of censorship is not only politically incorrect but also, and above all, inefficient. What must be done is to arm people's consciousness, to give them the ability to distance themselves critically. And to that effect I think that the most effective dam a country can have is its cultural heritage and the role that education, both in the school and at home, plays in inculcating values. I don't mean that we should close ourselves off from the world but that we should assimilate all the good things the world has to offer from the standpoint of our own reality. José Martí said it a long time ago. 'Let the world be grafted onto our republics but the trunk must grow in our republics.'[67]

75   The best antidote 'to *Rambo*, *Forrest Gump*, Disneyland and the whole Yankee hoax, and to the political, economic and social model represented by these symbols', is Cuban national culture which 'anticipates the Bolivarian homeland and the authentically universal homeland' – argues Abel Prieto, Minister of Culture of Cuba, who consequently thinks that the 'most serious "ideological problem"' related to culture is precisely 'the lack of culture'.[68]

76   It is interesting to know that even in the United States itself a dissident culture has arisen which, according to Chomsky, has grown enormously since the 1960s,[69] and which has gained even more strength of late because of the huge mobilisation against the war in Iraq.

Fragmenting strategy

77   And then on top of all this there is the fragmenting strategy of neo-liberalism, which knows that a divided society – where diverse minority groups are unable to form themselves into a majority which questions the existing hegemony – is the most appropriate formula for reproducing the system.

78   This strategy is used not only on the workers – in an attempt 'to deconstruct the labour force into an aggregate of differentiated actors or subjects separated the one from the other'[70] – but on society as a whole.

79   The Argentinean researcher Alberto Binder presents a detailed discussion of this strategy in his article on the fragmented society.[71]

80   According to Binder, what this strategy sets out to do is build or manufacture isolated social groups or minorities which war amongst themselves, thus allowing the hegemonic groups to maintain *horizontal social control*.

81   The basis for keeping these groups isolated amongst themselves or subject to contradictory relations is a conscious effort to disorient them about their possible common interests, thus making it impossible for these minorities to enter into collective struggles. A fragmented society implies a minority – and sometimes an entire society – that has lost the way towards its own national goal.

82   This policy of *social disorientation* acts, basically, on three levels: (a) the *atomisation* of society into groups with little power; (b) the orientation of these groups towards exclusive and partial ends, which don't encourage *combination*; (c) the elimination of their ability to negotiate and make '*pacts*'.

83   In order to achieve these aims people must be prevented from creating spaces where they can set goals which look beyond each particular group, that is, aims which other groups might share, which could lead to potential agreements and alliances. Hence, the prediction about the death of ideologies becomes a fundamental part of this strategy. Society is no longer understood and analysed as a whole; therefore social utopias which create meeting spaces for different groups disappear. This also encourages a 'shipwreck' culture; a culture of 'I'm all right, Jack' which discounts any kind of collective solution.

84   This is an overall power strategy whose aim is to smash society to pieces and make it absolutely impossible to build the concept of a majority; it sets the scene for the limited or restricted democracy we have analysed earlier.

The military danger

85   On the other hand, in spite of the end of the Cold War and the absence of any military powers that can endanger the capitalist system, the arms race

and the accumulation of more and more sophisticated arsenals of exter-mination are still going on.[72]

86   In this context, the 11 September 2001 terrorist attack on the Twin Towers in New York, which cost thousands of innocent lives including those of hundreds of Latin Americans who were working there, was like manna from heaven for the US government; it allowed it 'to exploit this crime and silence those both inside and outside the United States who opposed its imperialist ambitions'.[73]

87   A very clever media campaign was used to create a veritable collective psychosis which was to prepare the ground for a great worldwide 'crusade' against terrorism.

88   As Samir Amin says, a new McCarthyism was born. Its aim was to 'satanise any opposition to the dictates of ruling capital in the name of "homeland security" and the "war on terrorism"'.[74] What they are doing, as Chesnais says, 'is creating a new global counterrevolutionary Holy Alliance'.[75]

89   In the name of security they place restrictions on the constitutional freedoms and guarantees which are so important to US citizens: corres-pondence and telephone calls are subject to government surveillance; one should not be surprised when people are placed under surveillance as if they were suspects, especially if they look in the least bit Asian or have spoken publicly against the current policy of the US government. The authorities have gone to the extreme of recommending that everyone become police informants and denounce any suspicious individual. There is strict censorship which 'selects what the public should or should not know about the war ... only "authorised pictures" are published or broadcast'.[76]

90   Afghanistan was the first step, then followed Iraq and now they are announcing that Iran is the next target in 'this all-out war against terrorism', that is, against those the United States considers to be 'a potential enemy'. 'The same seven ton bombs which destroyed Afghan cities could explode tomorrow in the Colombian jungles.'[77] Were not the Colombian guerrilla groups (FARC-EP and the ELN) on the list of terrorist groups that appeared when the campaign first began?

91   Terrorism will not be eliminated by creating 'a united front against terrorism' such as the United States is trying to impose across the board. The only thing that will get rid of terrorism for ever will be the

elimination of its causes. Therefore what Samir Amin proposes makes much more sense: 'a single front against international social injustice. This front', when it becomes a reality, 'could render the desperate acts of the system's victims useless and, by the same token, impossible.'[78]

92   This international front against injustice and against war could unite activists from the South and North around definite aims, those of trying to prevent wars that are being prepared, of supporting the resistance in countries that have been invaded by the United States and its allies, and of exposing the campaigns that use the label 'terrorist' to try to satanise both national liberation groups, those that fight against exploitation and injustice in the Third World and the anti-globalisation movements in the North.[79]

93   Such a great front built at the grassroots level would be capable of gluing together growing sectors of the population using simple concrete language: capable of uniting the anti-war struggle with the day-to-day concerns of people – which are of course different in different places – and of fusing the enthusiasm of the young with the experience of previous generations.[80]

The phenomenon of imperialism has not disappeared, but has taken on new forms

94   Taking action in the bipolar world which existed when the Cuban revolution triumphed – when the socialist bloc gave rearguard support to revolutionary movements and generally served to keep capitalist abuse of Western workers in check – is not the same as to take action in today's unipolar world, where there is no opponent to the developed capitalist bloc.

95   Acting in a world where workers wielded much greater negotiating power – because strikes could inflict serious damage on employer interests – is not the same as acting in the world of the information revolution, when industries are mobile and wage or tax increases in the country where they operate may lead capital to emigrate to a more 'user-friendly' country.

96   According to Noam Chomsky, there is a type of virtual senate of financial speculators. If a country decides to put greater emphasis on its social development programmes, 'the virtual senate can vote

instantaneously [against those policies] by withdrawing enormous sums of capital from the country'.[81] This can have disastrous consequences for a small country.

97   The phenomenon of imperialism has not disappeared but has taken on a new shape.

Chapter 2
Profound Discontent
Among Much of Humankind

98   No matter how one interprets the magnitude of the changes the world is going through today, there is no doubt that the impact of the most recent scientific-technical revolution on the political, social, economic and cultural spheres has been enormous.

99   However, these new horizons that seem to be opening up for humankind are paradoxically accompanied by a great feeling of discontent among many people. We live in troubled times, full of confusion and uncertainty.

100   Not only has Soviet-style socialism failed, but capitalism has also demonstrated a surprising capacity to adapt to new circumstances and to avail itself of the new technological and scientific advances. Socialist nations, on the other hand, after having achieved a significant level of economic development, began slipping toward stagnation and the disaster we all know about. In addition, social democratic governments and their welfare states in Europe began to experience difficulties: stalled economic growth, inflation and inefficient production.

101   Meanwhile Latin America, after the painful structural adjustments of the 1980s (now known as 'the lost decade'), has begun to join the new global economy, though as we've seen at a very high price: a large segment of its population 'has been excluded from the dynamic sectors of the economy, as producers and consumers. In some cases, peoples, countries and regions have turned to the informal local economy (black and grey market), illegal exports and smuggling as a means of compensating for this exclusion.'[82]

Decline in the standard of living

102   The decline in the standard of living of the majority of the planet's population, including increasingly broad sectors of the middle class (some have referred to this process as 'the globalisation of poverty'[83]) is alarming. The threat of unemployment is a constant concern in both poor and developed countries. Social and organisational fragmentation 'has reached its highest level'.[84] The deterioration of the environment is a threat to future generations. 'Galloping corruption' has produced a widespread demoralising effect.[85] The threat of war, including nuclear war, continues and will continue to exist – in spite of the progress of the march toward peace, détente, and disarmament – until the causes that spring from the capitalist nature of the ruling international and socio-economic order are eradicated.

103   Neo-liberal policies carried out by big transnational capital backed up by huge military might and media power – whose hegemonic centre is the United States – have not only failed to solve these problems but have also exacerbated misery and social exclusion to a frightening degree, while wealth is becoming concentrated in fewer and fewer hands.

104   Those suffering from the economic consequences of neo-liberalism include – in addition to the traditional sectors of the urban and rural working classes – the poor and marginalised, the impoverished middle strata, a constellation of owners of small and medium-sized businesses, the informal sector, medium and small rural producers, most professionals, the legions of unemployed, workers in cooperatives, pensioners, the police and the lower ranks of the army.[86] However, we should also include not only those who are affected economically, but also all those who are discriminated against and oppressed by the system: women, young people, children, the elderly, indigenous peoples, people of African descent, certain religious groups, homosexuals, etcetera: in other words, most people in our countries.

105   However, although it is true that our enemies are very powerful, we can also see that the majority of people are manifesting an increasingly forceful rejection of the neo-liberal model imposed on the world because this model is incapable of solving our people's most pressing problems.

106   Some of the sectors that oppose neo-liberal globalisation have transformed themselves into powerful movements. These include the women's, the indigenous, the environmental, the consumer and the Human Rights movements. These differ in many ways from the classic labour movement because of the nature of their platforms. They place strong emphasis on the particular interest represented (such as the environment or women), on appealing to a broad spectrum of classes and generations, 'on concrete forms of action, and on organisational structures that are less hierarchical and more network-based than in the past'.[87]

107   On other occasions, one-off actions are initiated by new social actors. For example, young people's ability to mobilize is amazing – they organise for the most part via electronic networking – their aim being to repudiate neo-liberalism in its present form and to fight back against typical neo-liberal constraints.

The new international cycle

Seattle: a network way of organising

108   This generalised suffering and discontent has caused more and more generalised reactions. I agree with Hardt and Negri that a 'new international cycle finally emerged around the issues of globalization in the late 1990s'.[88] The protests at the WTO summit in Seattle in 1999 were the coming-out party of the new cycle of struggles.

109   'The pinnacle of this cycle of struggles thus far, at least in quantitative terms, were the coordinated protests against the US-led war in Iraq on February 15, 2003, in which millions of people marched in cities throughout the world. The war represented the ultimate instance of the global power against which the cycle of struggles had formed; the organizational structures and communication that the struggles had established made possible a massive, coordinated mobilization of common expressions against the war.'[89]

110   According to Hardt and Negri this 'new global cycle of struggles is a mobilization of the common that takes the form of an open, distributed network, in which no center exerts control and all nodes express themselves freely'.[90]

111   Unfortunately, once the mobilising episode or event is over, these militant outbursts in favour of a different world usually fade away, because there is no organisation capable of leading them, keeping them united and able to overcome their heterogeneity. Perhaps this lack of permanence is because they are very new, or because their militancy is less committed or different to previous kinds, or because they have less physical space for their meetings and organisation. Since these are very young movements, it could be that the potential contribution the different actors could make is not yet well defined.[91]

Upsurge of struggles in Latin America

112   Nevertheless, in addition to this cycle of world struggles, a new cycle of national struggles has also arisen simultaneously in Latin America. When President Hugo Chávez won the elections in 1998 he stood practically alone; he was the only leader putting forward a project that was an alternative to neo-liberalism. Today what the enemy has called the 'red tide' is advancing across almost all Latin American countries. It has not only taken over the government in countries such as Brazil, Argentina, Uruguay, Bolivia, Chile – but progress is being made in the people's struggles of resistance to neo-liberalism in Ecuador, Colombia and Costa Rica. Local leaders and a central leadership have indeed played an important role in this Latin American phenomenon. Without diminishing the huge role played by popular movements and especially indigenous movements, one may assert that Evo Morales would have found it difficult to become president of Bolivia if Movimiento al Socialismo (MAS) had not existed.

Concepts of multitude and social people

113   The concept of multitude used by Hardt and Negri encompasses all those sectors included in Helio Gallardo's concept of the social people; these form themselves into a multitude when that 'internally distinct and multiple social subject is capable of acting in common'.[92]

114   Years earlier Helio Gallardo had used the term 'social people'[93] to refer to all those sectors which suffer the consequences of today's

savage capitalism. This term includes not only those who could be called impoverished from a socio-economic point of view, but also those who are impoverished in their subjectivity.

Chapter 3
Towards the Creation of an Alternative Social Bloc

115 'The profundity of the crisis and the breadth and variety of the affected sectors ... make for a scenario highly conducive to the construction of an extremely broad based alternative social bloc with an enormous force given that its potential members – they include most of the population – are legion.'[94]

116   In view of the situation of growing discontent and neo-liberalism's fragmenting strategy described above there can be no doubt that the Left's strategic task is to unite the growing but scattered social opposition into one vast column, one torrent, and to transform it into a force able to deal a decisive blow to the ruling system.

The need to rebuild the Left so that it can become the glue that sticks the social opposition together

117 For this broad convergence of sectors and forces we are proposing to become a real possibility, it is crucial that we are able to rebuild the Left, which is not exactly equal to the task just now.

118   But what does Left mean?

119   By the Left, I mean the array of forces that oppose the capitalist system and its profit motive and which are fighting for an alternative humanist, solidarity-filled society, a socialist society, the building blocks of which are the interests of the working classes. This society would be 'free from material poverty and the spiritual wretchedness engendered by capitalism'.[95]

120   The Left, therefore, is not only the Left that is organised in Left parties or organisations; it also includes social actors and movements who are trying to create autonomous spaces. These are very often more dynamic and combative; they identify with the above ideals, but are not members of any political party or organisation. The first group includes some who prefer to build their strength by using institutions to bring about change and some who opt for revolutionary guerrilla warfare; the second group includes those who want to create autonomous social movements and various types of networks.

121   To simplify, I have decided to call the first group 'the party Left'; and the second group 'the social Left'. I am convinced that only by uniting the militant efforts of the whole gamut of Left groups will we be able to build a huge anti-neo-liberal social bloc; a bloc in which all those suffering the consequences of today's brutal capitalism will converge.

The first strategic task: coordinating the political and social Left

122   The first task, then, will be to coordinate the party Left and the social Left, and, based on that, to arrive at that greater confluence which unites all social discontent into a single torrent.

123   Although it is really important that the different sectors of the Left converge, I do not believe this aim can be achieved in a voluntarist way, creating coalitions from above which might be doomed to end up as simply a pile of acronyms. The vertical vanguard–masses relationship must also be overcome.

A new strategy for the anti-capitalist struggle would make coordination easier

124   I think that if, instead, we apply a new strategy of anti-capitalist struggle, we could create conditions more favourable to coordination.

125   But, what would this strategy be?

126   It would be a strategy which is aware of the important social, political, economic and cultural transformations that have taken place in the world recently; which understands that the new forms of capitalism's domination go far beyond the economic and state arenas to infiltrate all the nooks and crannies of society, changing the conditions of struggle.

127   Today more than ever we have to go up against 'not only the ruling class's political coercion apparatuses but also its hegemony over important popular sectors, its cultural control over society and the ideological subordination of the dominated classes … we have to be able to identify not only the coercive power exercised by the state, its legislative and repressive activities, but also the mechanisms and institutions which are present in civil society' and which lead to the people accepting the capitalist social order.[96] Propaganda is to bourgeois democracy 'what the bludgeon is to the totalitarian state'.[97]

128   As Carlos Ruiz says,[98] we must begin by understanding that our challenge is to formulate revolutionary strategy while living in a bourgeois democracy that enjoys sufficient *mass loyalty* to sustain itself without having to resort to repression – what's more, broad sectors of the people are quite happy with the way the capitalists run things.

129   Merely talking up alternative society is not enough. Today *domination assumes more complex forms*; there are *powerful extra-state factors* which produce and reproduce the current *dismemberment of popular sectors* and which attempt to discredit Left thought and the Left's project in the eyes of the public; all of these factors demand that the Left practise what it preaches. This is only possible if it develops *alternatives to capitalism created by the people* that shatter the logic of profit and the relationships which this imposes; tries to install a logic of humanism and solidarity in the localities and spaces that are in the hands of the Left; backs struggles that go beyond simple economistic demands – even though these are necessarily a part of such struggles – and advances an alternative social project; fosters authentic degrees of popular power and democracy that are tangibly superior to bourgeois democracy.[99] We have to fight for a new type of democracy from below, for those below.

130   Only a strategy of this type generates *a permanent and growing struggle* that can overcome the *deceptive dynamics of 'episodic' victories.*

Building a broad anti-neo-liberal social and political bloc

131   This bloc should provide space, as stated earlier, for 'all those who suffer the consequences of the system and are willing to commit themselves first to the struggle to hold those consequences in check and then to try to reverse them'.[100]

132   In order to coordinate the interests of such diverse actors we must be able to formulate concrete, limited demands that give priority to points of convergence.

133   We need to design a programme which unites all the 'losers' and all those harmed by neo-liberalism.[101] Its aims would include halting the development of neo-liberalism and offering concrete alternatives to today's serious problems.

Capitalist sectors in direct contradiction to the transnationals

134   It could also include capitalist sectors whose business activity has entered into an objective contradiction with transnational capital. We are not referring here to bourgeois sectors capable of carrying through their own national development project, but to sectors that have no alternative but to insert themselves into a popular, national project if they are to survive, being motivated to do so by a popular government's offer of credit and by the thought of the large internal market resulting from the social policies of such a government.

135   When this problem is analysed the matter of the balance of power must not be forgotten. As long as the bourgeoisie feels powerful and thinks it can control things either through the ballot box or with arms it will certainly not be willing to collaborate with a revolutionary project that runs counter to the logic of capital.

136   One example of how some sectors of the bourgeoisie join a project to create a country that is an alternative to neo-liberalism is that of Venezuela. What could the Venezuelan bourgeoisie do after it had been thrice defeated? Its attempted coup in April 2002 failed; its employers' strike at the end of that year and beginning of 2003 didn't achieve its purpose; nor was it able to get rid of Chávez through the August 2004 referendum.

137   The control of political power, exchange controls, a correct credit policy which gives capitalists loans provided they accept certain conditions set by the government (for example, that they produce for the domestic market and create jobs; that they pay their taxes; that they collaborate with the surrounding communities) are the formulas the Bolivarian government uses to get the owners of medium and small

Venezuelan businesses to commit themselves to working with the government's programme whose central focus is the elimination of poverty. The sectors who collaborate are precisely those which have been most affected by neo-liberal globalisation.

138   These agreements naturally entail a risk. The logic of capital will also try to assert itself. There will be a constant struggle to see who will defeat whom. We are at the beginning of a long process.

139   And, mindful of the fact that we are looking at two antagonistic economic models, it is of vital importance that a very large share of state resources is allocated to financing and developing the public sector. This is because control of strategic industries is the best way to ensure that the new humanist, solidarity-based logic triumphs and that the national development plan aimed at eliminating poverty is carried out.

PART II
The Crisis of 'Party' and Why We Need a New Left Political Culture

Chapter 4
Crisis of Theory

140 The Latin American Left is not really in any state to undertake this task
of coordination because of its state of crisis and because its forces are
scattered.

141   This crisis encompasses, basically, three areas: *theory*; *programme*, which
is related to the crisis of credibility of politics and politicians; and the
organic crisis, which we shall explain in more detail in this book.

Threefold origin

142 As I understand it, the Latin American Left's crisis of theory has a
threefold origin. The first is its *historical incapacity to construct its own system
of thought* – one that would start out with an analysis of the real situation
in each Latin American country, identifying a tradition of struggle and the
potential for change. With the exception of a handful of efforts to do so,[102]
the tendency was rather to extrapolate from analytical models that refer
to other parts of the world. Previous analyses were made using European
parameters: for example, Latin America was considered to be a feudal
system – when in reality it was a dependent capitalist one – or a
European class analysis was applied to countries whose populations were
mostly indigenous, which caused people to overlook the importance of
ethno-cultural factors.[103]

143   In the second place, the Left hasn't been capable of carrying out a
rigorous study of various socialist experiences – their successes as well as
failures – and that is in part owing to the fact that few comprehensive,

systematic studies on these experiences have been widely publicised.[104] Nor has a serious analysis been made of the reasons for the defeat of these experiences.

144 However, the most important explanation for the crisis of theory is the lack of a critical study of late twentieth-century capitalism – the capitalism of the electronic information revolution, of globalisation and financial wars. I'm not talking about partial studies of given aspects of contemporary capitalist society (which do indeed exist),[105] but of a rigorous, comprehensive study such as Marx made of capitalism at the time of the industrial revolution.

145 For example, how is the concept of surplus value – a central concept in Marx's critical analysis of capitalism – modified with the introduction of digital machines and robotics, on the one hand, and the current globalisation process, on the other? How does the introduction of new technologies into the labour process and into the whole economic process affect the technical and social relations of production and those of distribution and consumption? What changes have both the working class and the bourgeoisie undergone in an era where knowledge has come to represent a key element in the productive forces? How can Marxism be used to think about environmental and gender problems? How can we measure the human development that takes place through people's protagonistic participation in their social and cultural interactions? Where is globalisation headed and what will the consequences be? What are the elements that might make up a potential objective basis for transforming this mode of production?

146 An analysis of this type is essential, because an alternative society can only arise from the potentialities inherent in the society in which we live. And I cannot see a way to make such an analysis other than by using the scientific instrument Marx bequeathed us.

147 On the other hand, if we want to transform the world we must be capable of detecting the 'struggle potential' of various social sectors who will become the subject of social change. What is that potential today? Where should we be working? How should we organise them? What are the contradictions of the system? What is its weakest link?

148 We will only be able to give a serious answer to these questions if we make a scientific analysis of the society in which we live.

A crisis of Marxism doesn't mean we have to deny Marx's contributions

149 Marxism has much to contribute to all these questions.

150   The crisis of Soviet socialism doesn't mean – as many bourgeois ideologues have triumphantly concluded – that we should necessarily question Marx's scientific contributions. Unfortunately, some sectors of the Left have been excessively susceptible to neo-liberalism's anti-Marxist propaganda, which unfairly blames Marx's theory for what happened in the Soviet socialist countries. Nobody, however, would blame a cookbook because someone turned the oven up too high and burnt the cake.

Chapter 5
Programmatic Crisis and the Crisis of Credibility

No plan for an alternative to capitalism

151 But this is not enough to explain the current situation. The Latin American Left is experiencing a profound *programmatic crisis* stemming from the crisis of theory previously described. Political action is bereft of models capable of providing it with understanding and direction, because most of the old models have collapsed and the new ones haven't yet 'set'. It has had enormous difficulty in designing a programme for change which is *able to absorb the data about the new global reality*[106] and which enables all the sectors affected by the existing system to flow together – creating the single torrent I have mentioned already in this analysis. We have more than enough diagnosis but no treatment is prescribed. We have been attempting to set sail without *a compass.*[107]

152 Nevertheless we cannot say that the Left comes up empty-handed with regard to programmatic questions; there *are* alternative proposals and practices, but they haven't yet taken shape as a fully worked-out, convincing project.

153 Prior to 1998, the Left won control of important local governments in several countries in Latin America, especially in Brazil and Uruguay. In those places, it began to carry out interesting social experiments from which we could learn a lot.

154 In addition, from 1998 on it has managed to form the governments in Venezuela, Chile, Brazil, Argentina, Uruguay, and most recently, Bolivia and, again, Chile. Throughout the region, Left forces and parties have

begun to win more representation in the parliaments of various countries.

155   The major reason for all this is nothing other than the growing popular discontent caused by neo-liberal measures, which affect more and more of the population.

156   But there is a danger that, once it has become the government, the Left limits itself to managing the crisis while continuing to implement the essential elements of neo-liberal economic policies: this is what some Left governments seem to be doing. This kind of behaviour is detrimental not only in as far as it fails to alleviate the suffering caused by the neo-liberal model as quickly as and to the degree needed, but also – and this is even more dangerous – in that it could annihilate the Left option for years to come.

157   There clearly is a lack of any theoretical work to systematise all these diverse experiences into something coherent that can be applied in other circumstances.

158   It is equally important to bear in mind that alternatives can't be worked out overnight – at a conference or in a working group – because any alternative in today's world must include increasingly complex technical considerations that require specialised knowledge. Moreover, right now the Latin American left has few spaces to do this job. It wasn't like that at the end of the 1960s and the beginning of the 1970s. At that time, spaces were created in the universities in several countries and many alternative projects and programmes were drawn up there.

Crisis of the credibility of politics and politicians

159   Along with this crisis of programmes and partly caused by it there is a crisis which, even if it is not a crisis of the Left *per se*, nevertheless has a huge impact on it; we could label it a crisis of the *credibility of politics and politicians*, including political parties. We live at a time when specifically political participation has decreased – a worldwide phenomenon – reorienting itself towards other directions and other forms of action.[108] There is growing popular scepticism about politics and politicians in general.

160   There are several reasons for this, which include the great constraints placed on democratic regimes today – those we have discussed above.

161   Two further elements must be added to those discussed above and these affect the Left directly.

The Right has appropriated the Left's language

162 First is the fact that the Right has appropriated the Left's language. The most flagrant examples occur in the Right's programmes. Words like reform, structural change, concern over poverty, and transition today form part of their anti-people, oppressive discourse. As Franz Hinkelammert says: 'the key words used by the popular opposition movements of the 1950s and 1960s have become key words for those who destroyed those movements with sword and fire'.[109] He adds: 'Night falls and all cats are grey. Everyone is against privilege; all want reforms and structural change. Everyone is also in favour of helping the poor.'[110]

Left parties have shifted to the Right

163 Second, the Left has lost credibility because its political practice fails to stand out from the usual practice of traditional parties, right, left or centre. Often it isn't just a case of their political practice or style not being very different: 'many of the remaining major parties of the Left have drifted so far past the center that they tend to become indistinguishable from the Right, cutting welfare, attacking unions, supporting and conducting foreign wars'.[111]

164 There is a climate of heightened indifference – and for a good reason. Ordinary people are fed up with the traditional political system and want something new, want changes, want new ways of doing politics; they want healthy politics, transparency and participation; they want to regain trust.[112]

165 'Indifference is ferocious,' according to Viviane Forrester, 'it is the most active, and without a doubt, the most powerful political party of all.' And the worst thing is that from the point of view of the ruling class, this 'general indifference is a bigger victory for the system than any partial support they manage to win'.[113]

166 This indifference and disappointment with politics and politicians, which is increasing daily, is not a serious problem for the Right, but it certainly is for the Left. The Right can perfectly easily do without political parties, as it demonstrated during the dictatorships, but the Left can't, as we shall prove a little later on.

Chapter 6
The Organic Crisis

There is no political subject equal to the new challenges

167 If there is anything seriously affecting the Left in the current world state of affairs it is not having a political subject able to tackle the new challenges. Past structures, habits, traditions and ways of doing politics are not responding to the demands engendered by the changes the world has undergone.

168 I completely agree with the assessment made by Chilean socialist leader Clodomiro Almeyda that the parties of the Left 'find themselves today in an obvious crisis, not only because their projects and programmes were deficient or lacking, but also – and in no small way – because of things to do with their organic nature, their relations with civil society, with identifying their present functions and how to carry them out'.

169 'This crisis of the existing institutions of Left political parties manifests itself both in the loss of their ability to attract and mobilise people – especially young people – and in the dysfunctionality of their present structures, customs, traditions, and ways of doing politics vis-à-vis the demands that social reality makes on a popular, socialist political actor in a process of substantive renewal.'[114]

170 Moreover, not only are existing institutions in crisis, but also – as Hardt and Negri say – the 'social base in labor unions and the industrial working class is no longer powerful enough to support the Left political parties'.[115]

171   This crisis also affects work with social movements and new social actors.

How copying the Bolshevik model led to deviations

172   I think that this crisis – which I call an organic crisis – has a lot to do with an uncritical copying of the Bolshevik model of the party.

173   But why was this model so attractive to Latin American Marxist political cadres and those in other parts of the world? We should remember that it had been an effective instrument for making the world's first successful revolution of the oppressed against the power of the ruling classes. It was thanks to it that heaven seemed to have been taken by storm.

174   According to the English historian Eric Hobsbawm, '"Lenin's party of a new type" [was] a formidable innovation of twentieth-century social engineering, comparable to the invention of Christian monastic and other orders in the Middle Ages. It gave even small organizations disproportionate effectiveness, because the party could command extraordinary devotion and self-sacrifice from its members, more than military discipline and cohesiveness, and a total concentration on carrying out party decisions at all costs.'[116]

175   But, unfortunately, this great feat of 'social engineering' which was so effective in Russia – a backward society with an autocratic political regime – was transferred mechanically to Latin America, a very different society. Moreover, it was transferred in a simplified, dogmatic form. What the majority of the Latin American Left learned was not Lenin's thought in all its complexity, but the simplistic version offered by Stalin.

176   For Lenin, it was absolutely clear that there is no universal formula. He always saw the party as the *political subject* par excellence of social transformation, as the instrument which would provide political direction to the class struggle – a struggle that always takes place under specific historical, political, and social conditions. He therefore believed that the party's organic structure should be adapted to the reality of each country, and modified according to the concrete demands of struggle.

177   These early ideas of Lenin were ratified at the Third Congress of the Communist International in 1921. In one of his works he argues that: 'There is no absolute form of organisation which is correct for

Communist Parties at all times. The conditions of the proletarian class struggle are constantly changing, and so the proletarian vanguard has always to be looking for effective forms of organisation. Equally, each party must develop its own special forms of organisation to meet the particular historically-determined conditions within the country.'[117]

178   Nevertheless, in spite of the International's instructions, Communist Parties in practice followed a single model, in spite of the differences between the countries where they were founded.

179   Besides, it seems to me that some of Lenin's basic ideas, which he thought were universally applicable, could, if applied uncritically, lead to mistakes and deviations.

180   One of these errors was to conceive the party as a *working-class* party because that is the only revolutionary class. Another error was to insist that every party had to call itself 'the Communist Party of ...' if it wanted to belong to the Communist International. Such assumptions were applied dogmatically by the Latin American section of the International, whose influence was extremely damaging. Its leaders devotedly copied formulas invented for an undifferentiated Third World and ignored the specificities of Latin American countries. We don't have to go too far back to be reminded of the problems José Carlos Mariátegui faced when he did not respect the International's decision about the name of the working-class party he founded in Peru; he called it the Socialist Party and not the Communist Party, a prerequisite for joining the International.

181   The acritical emphasis placed on the working class led to Latin American parties ignoring the specific characteristics of that continent's revolutionary social subject and failing to understand the role that indigenous people and Christians can play in revolutions in Latin America.

Viewing religion as the opiate of the people

182   Until the 1960s, the Latin American and Caribbean Left mechanically applied Marx's remark that religion in his time was 'the opium of the people'. This was because they identified Christianity with the hierarchy of the Catholic Church – owing to its support for the ruling class – and didn't consider Christianity's revolutionary potential in this region.

183   The Left paid no attention to the changes that began taking place in the Catholic Church with the Second Vatican Council (1962–5) and culminated in the Medellin Conference in 1968. It paid attention neither to the

appearance of Liberation Theology and Christian Base Communities nor to the deeds of Camilo Torres, a priest-guerrilla who died fighting with the National Liberation Army (ELN) in Colombia. These factors taken together began to change the unjustified negative view of the role that Christians can play in a revolutionary movement.[118]

Christians in the Sandinista Revolution

184 It was the Sandinistas who began to correct this situation. For their struggle against Somoza, the FSLN recruited young Christians who were working in the poor areas of the cities. The idea wasn't to take them away from the work they were doing but to introduce revolutionary influence into the ecclesiastical base organisations. The recruits were left in their base communities so that this higher commitment would result in political action in this milieu. When asked to join the FSLN, they were never asked to make a choice between their Christian faith and their membership in the Front. If the Sandinistas had not posed the question of FSLN membership in these terms they would have remained a very small group of people.[119]

185 It was always the Sandinistas' official, principled position that there should be complete respect for religious beliefs. They fought against any signs of sectarianism and discrimination against believers that appeared.

186 Many Christians have been and are members of the FSLN, and some of them are even priests; as well as being rank-and-file members, priests have been members of the Sandinista Assembly and held top-level political responsibilities.

187 The FSLN officially recognised the support of Christians in a public statement in October 1980 – the first such recognition from a revolutionary party in power: 'we the Sandinistas confirm that our experience shows that when Christians, bolstered by their faith, are capable of responding to the people and history's needs, it is their very beliefs which push them into revolutionary militancy. Our experience has shown us that it is possible to be both a believer and a revolutionary and that there is not an irresolvable contradiction between the two things.'[120]

Neglect of ethno-cultural factors

188 Similarly, the situation of indigenous people was neglected by the Latin American Left for decades (with a few exceptions, such Mariátegui and

Haya de la Torre). The application of a strict class analysis to the indigenous peasantry meant they were considered to be an exploited social class and should fight for their land like any other peasants, thus ignoring the importance of the ethno-cultural factor with ancestral traditions of resistance to oppression. Today, the Latin American revolutionary movement has come to understand two things: one, that it must respect the language, customs, religious beliefs and cultural norms of indigenous peoples if it doesn't want to be identified as an ally of the oppressor; and, two, that there is immense revolutionary potential – stemming from their ancestral traditions of resistance to oppression – pent up in these economically exploited and culturally oppressed peoples.[121]

189   The recent presidential elections in Bolivia, which gave a clear majority to Evo Morales, an indigenous peasant union leader from Cochabamba in a predominantly indigenous country, are the best proof of the increasingly important role that this social sector is playing.

A conception of revolution as storming the bastions of state power

190   Another of the Left's theoretical assumptions was the conception of revolution as 'storming the bastions of state power'. This stemmed from a conception that *located power only in the state*. Parties inspired by the Bolshevik Party concentrated all their efforts on preparing to storm these bastions and ignored other aspects of the struggle, such as the task of culturally transforming the people's consciousness. This was relegated to something to be done after power was seized.

Not setting enough store by democracy

191   Moreover, for many years Left organisations, influenced by the importance Lenin attributed to the dictatorship of the proletariat, dismissed another of his premises: that socialism should be conceived of as the most democratic society possible, as opposed to bourgeois society which is democratic for a minority only.

192   Comparing socialism and capitalism, Lenin said that under the latter democracy only exists 'for the rich and for a tiny layer of the proletariat', whereas in the transition phase or under socialism, democracy is 'almost complete, limited only by the need to crush bourgeois resistance'. Under communism where the ruling principle is 'from each according to his

ability, to each according to his need', democracy will be, to all intents and purposes, complete.[122]

193   These parties did not understand that the importance attributed by Lenin to the subject of the dictatorship could be explained by the need to defeat a counter-revolution which did not accept the revolution's rules of the game for the new society and which, in order to recover the power it had lost, turned to the world counter-revolution for help. The opposition's fierce and bloody reaction obliged the Soviet government to use a firm hand.

Other mistakes and deviations

194   But there are other mistakes, deviations and absences[123] which cannot be attributed to the theories mentioned above and which have led to movements and social actors roundly rejecting Left parties.

Vanguardism

195   One of the Latin American Left's most negative attitudes was to proclaim itself to be either the vanguard of the revolutionary process or the vanguard of the working class, even though this class was virtually non-existent in some Latin American countries. For a long time, it was virtually unthinkable that other organisations could be equally or more revolutionary than they were, or potential allies with whom power could be shared.

196   In addition, they didn't understand that being the vanguard is not something a party bestows upon itself but something that is earned through struggle and that there can't be a vanguard without a rearguard.

197   They certainly failed to understand the distinction Lenin established between the moment in which the party and the revolutionary organisation is formed – during which the leadership cadres are trained – and the moment when it manages to acquire the authentic ability to lead the class struggle. Most Latin American Left organisations never managed to acquire this 'authentic ability to lead'.

198   Each organisation fought over the right to be called the most revolutionary, the most just, and all the other accolades: what mattered most was the sect, the T-shirt, and not the revolution. That's how sectarianism arose and most parties fell prey to it.

199   The political-military organisations thought all parties which were not engaged in the armed struggle were reformist. And some of these non-armed-struggle parties (especially the Communist Parties) claimed that, by definition, there could be no one further to the left than they were – disparagingly branding those who *were* to their left as 'ultraleftists'.

Verticalism and authoritarianism

200   The vertical style of leadership – which translated into an attempt to lead from above, handing down to the rank and file lines of action drawn up by the political leadership – was common practice. The leadership cadres were the people who knew where to go, and therefore decisions about everything that was done were handed down ready-made from above. It was assumed that anything the leadership thought was right, and therefore that the members simply had to carry out the instructions handed down. Such leaders took no trouble to convince people of the correctness of their proposals.

201   Those who determined the line were the leadership cadres, and the tendency was to create mechanisms which allowed them to keep control in their hands by, in practice, denying access to new blood.

Social movements as mere transmission belts

202   There is a close connection between the above and the existence of a tendency to consider grassroots movements as there to be manipulated, mere channels through which to hand down the party line. Leadership of the movement, jobs in the leadership bodies, the platform for struggle, everything in fact, was decided on by the top ranks of the party and then the line to be followed by the social movement in question was handed down. The movement was not able to take part in making decisions about the matters which most concerned them.

203   To support this position, the leaderships have used Lenin's thesis about unions at the beginning of the Russian Revolution, when a very close relationship seemed to exist between the working class, the vanguard party and the state.

204   However, few know – as a result of the ahistorical and incomplete way in which Lenin has been read – that this notion was abandoned by the Russian leader towards the end of his life when, in the midst of the New Economic Policy (NEP) and its consequences in the labour sphere, he

foresaw the possible contradictions which could arise between workers in state companies and the managers of those companies. He argued that unions should defend the interests of the working class against the employers, using, if necessary, the strike – which would not, in a proletarian state, be aimed at destroying that state but only at correcting its bureaucratic deviations.[124]

205　　This change went unnoticed by Marxist-Leninist parties which, until very recently, understood the metaphor of the transmission belt to describe accurately Lenin's thesis on the relationship between the party and the social organisation.

An over-reliance on theory, dogma and strategy

206　Another problem was that theory was excessively overvalued. This translated into an over-reliance on theory and a tendency to be dogmatic. There was a tendency to make general theoretical analyses or to copy foreign models, and an inability to explain how concrete processes worked.

207　　For decades, generally speaking, the Left imported prefabricated models from other revolutionary experiences, and, most of the time, parties developed their strategies not by trying to find their own road, tailored to the country's own conditions, but by patching something together with bits copied from strategies developed in all kinds of revolutionary experiences all over the world.

208　　It is important to remember that both the 26th of July Movement in Cuba and the Sandinista Front in Nicaragua were able to win their struggles because, among other things, they were able to take further an existing tradition of national liberation struggle. They made the revolution, as someone said, in Spanish and not in Russian. Their spiritual fathers were Martí and Sandino. This has also happened in the recent revolutionary process in Venezuela. Its leader, Hugo Chávez, has known how to resuscitate the thinking of Simón Bolívar, Simón Rodríguez, (Bolívar's teacher) and Ezequiel Zamora.

209　　What a difference between this and the profile many Latin American Leftist organisations had! What does the sickle on the red flag of many communist parties mean to our people? What do Ho Chi Minh or even Che Guevara – names that were adopted by some guerrilla movements – mean to Guatemalan indigenous peoples?

210　　One result of this was the strategist deviation. Grand strategic goals were formulated – the struggle for national liberation and socialism – but no concrete analysis was made of the existing situation, the starting point. Among other things, this was the result of the erroneous belief that revolutionary conditions existed throughout Latin America – all that was needed was to light the spark and the whole prairie would burst into flame. This led to slogan-based political agitation which was of no help in building a popular social force.

211　Debates were therefore sterile. It was difficult to make progress if only general, very theoretical questions were discussed and concrete circumstances were never analysed. In fact, many of these theoretical debates resulted in splits because they divided the various forces even more.

212　This led to two errors which were often interrelated: on the one hand, it was believed that the path toward unity should avoid theoretical debates; on the other there was an exclusive emphasis on practice (*practicismo*) which rejected any attempt to theorise about reality.

213　Over-reliance on theory and dogmatism both existed in the most widely disparate branches of the Left, in traditional Leftist parties as well as in the self-proclaimed revolutionary Left, though this relationship was not symmetrical. The latter was inspired by the genuinely Latin American process of the Cuban Revolution and tried to find its own path.

214　I do not think it is particularly bold to make this claim: that the absence of a well-argued theoretical-historical analysis of conditions in individual countries and on the sub-continent as a whole is one of the reasons why – when hegemonism and sectarianism have been overcome and there is a genuine desire for unity – it has still been difficult for Latin American revolutionary forces to move towards unity.

Subjectivism

215　Unfortunately, this lack of concrete analysis also meant that these parties made extremely subjective assessments of the correlation of forces in a given situation. There was a tendency for leadership cadres filled with revolutionary passion to confuse their desires with reality. No objective analysis of the situation was made, so they tended to underestimate the enemy's and overestimate the party's own strength.

216　In addition, leaders tended to confuse the mood of the most radical party members with that of the rank and file. Many political leaders were in the habit of making generalisations about the mood of the people based upon their own experiences garnered in the region or sector where they operated, on their guerrilla front or, more generally, from those around them – who were usually the most radicalised elements.

217   The view of Chile held by people who worked with the more radicalised sectors of the population in that country was different from that of those who did their political work with the less politicised sectors. The revolutionary cadres who worked in a combative poor neighbour-hood in Chile didn't see things the same way as those who worked among the middle classes. The same thing occurred in countries where there were war zones and political spaces. The guerrilla fighters who engaged in confrontations with the enemy and who, thanks to their military victories, gained control over certain zones tended to believe that the revolutionary process was more advanced than did those activists who operated in legal spheres in the major urban centres, where the ruling regime's ideological power and military control were much greater.

218   The only guarantee against committing these errors is to ensure that leaders themselves are capable of making an evaluation of the situation that does not depend on their mood but on their ability to take the pulse of the masses, the enemy and the international situation. Once they have done this, it is essential to decide on the lines of action that enable them to capitalise on the situation.

219   It is important that the top leaders learn to listen and that they avoid projecting their preconceived notions when meeting with intermediate and rank-and-file leaders. If they don't know how to listen – which requires a healthy dose of revolutionary modesty – and if they are given false information, what then happens is that the lines of action handed down do not correspond to the real potential for mobilisation.

220   Moreover, there has been a tendency for the Left to deceive itself, to falsify the figures about demonstrations, meetings, strikes, or the forces that each organisation has – all of which later results in lines of action that are not correct because they are based upon false information.

221   The Left deceived itself not only about numbers but also about the assessment of actions it proposed taking. If the objective to have a given number of representatives elected to parliament was not attained, this was not admitted. Instead the leadership would always try to present the outcome as a victory – saying, for example, that more votes had been registered than in the previous election. Or, if a general strike was called

and there were only partial strikes, no setback was acknowledged; instead there was talk about how successful the strike had been compared to previous actions of this kind because there had been an increase in the number of workers who didn't go to work.

222   In the 1970s, the awful blows the Left received and the upsurge in the Central American revolutionary process meant that left-wing leaders matured quickly. They began to become aware of all of these errors and deviations. I realise, however, that becoming aware of something doesn't mean it is always immediately incorporated into political practice. There's nothing unusual about that, because a certain amount of time is required to overcome the habits of decades, and for changes to be assimilated by mid-level and rank-and-file cadres.

Chapter 7
The Theory Underlying This Concept of Party

223   In the previous chapter we have referred to several errors and deviations which plagued the Latin American Left because its organisational approach was inspired by the Bolshevik model of the party. We ought to ask why these shortcomings have been repeated by so many Left organisations and why they continue to exist, even though they are now acknowledged to be negative attitudes.

224   Althusser liked to say it is not enough to acknowledge errors; their causes must be understood if they are to be overcome. And my search for these causes has led me to conclude that the roots of most of the deviations I have mentioned lie in the famous thesis about the need to introduce socialist theory into the labour movement from without because the spontaneous development of this movement can never produce socialism.

Some explanation for these errors: Kautsky's thesis

The almighty role of the ruling ideology

225   This thesis, taken by Lenin from Kautsky, was given a theoretical basis by Louis Althusser in his writings on the Marxist conception of ideology and was repeated by me in *The Elementary Concepts of Historical Materialism*[125] and in Popular Education Notebook No. 8, *The Party: Vanguard of the Proletariat*.[126]

226   In his pre-1979 writings on the subject, Althusser argued that all ideology was necessarily a deformed view of reality and served the ruling class; and, although he accepted the existence of different ideological

tendencies – bourgeois, petty-bourgeois, proletarian – he argued that the latter were subordinate to ruling-class ideology. These arguments led him to conclude that the working class could only be liberated from the domination of bourgeois ideology and manage to acquire class consciousness with the help of the science of history. The labour movement could not attain class consciousness on its own, so it must be introduced from outside.[127]

227   Looking at the problem this way, the distinction made by Marx between a class in itself and a class for itself was assimilated into the distinction between ideological consciousness and scientific consciousness, and science was what allowed passage from the first to the second.

Premises of Kautsky's thesis

228   Before continuing, let us look at exactly what Kautsky says in the text referred to by Lenin. In the Austrian Social-Democrat Party's new draft programme, Kautsky argued thus. *First*, economic development and the class struggle don't, on their own, raise consciousness about the necessity for socialism. Proof of that is that England, the country most highly developed capitalistically, is more remote than any other from this consciousness. *Second*, socialism and the class struggle arise side by side and not one out of the other, and they arise under different conditions. *Third*, Modern socialist consciousness can arise only on the basis of profound scientific knowledge. *Fourth*, the vehicle of science is not the proletariat but the bourgeois intelligentsia. *Fifth*, sectors of the bourgeois intelligentsia communicate this to the more intellectually advanced proletarians, who introduce it into the proletarian class struggle wherever the conditions allow that to be done.

229   Conclusion: socialist consciousness is something imported into the proletarian class struggle from without and not something that arises spontaneously within it.

230   I find it difficult to argue against these statements that history has confirmed. I think the problem arises when we identify socialist consciousness with class consciousness.

Interpreting Lenin

231   There are texts by Lenin that lend themselves to this reading. There is one that argues that the spontaneous development of the working-class

movement leads to subordination to bourgeois ideology: that it is out of the question to think that workers can develop an *independent ideology* – in other words, class consciousness – *as their movement progresses*. There is only *bourgeois ideology or socialist ideology*. There is no third ideology.[128] And this socialist ideology can only be arrived at when somebody else imports socialism, in other words, Marxist theory, into the labour movement.

232   In other writings, however, Lenin recognises that practical experience plays a fundamental role in creating class consciousness. According to him, 'the self-knowledge of the working class is indissolubly bound up, not solely with a fully clear theoretical understanding – or rather, not so much with the theoretical as with the practical understanding – of the relationships between all the various classes of modern society, acquired through the experience of political life'.[129] This formation of consciousness advances enormously in revolutionary periods through the *march of revolutionary events*, since revolutions expose the true interests of the various classes, whereas demagoguery can deceive the people in peaceful times.[130]

233   'During a revolution', Lenin wrote in the midst of the Russian revolutionary process of February 1902, 'millions and tens of millions of people learn in a week more than they do in a year of ordinary, somnolent life. For at the time of a sharp turn in the life of an entire people it becomes particularly clear what aims the various classes of the people are pursuing, what strength they possess, and what methods they use.'[131]

234   Yet in spite of Lenin's writings, and his demonstration of the importance of revolutionary practice in creating consciousness, the thesis that was popularised among the masses – and I was one of those who popularised it – was the one that put the emphasis on the need to import Marxist theory into the labour movement because the spontaneous development of this movement cannot help but lead to subordination to bourgeois ideology.[132]

Deformation of Kautsky's thesis

235   The simplified, incorrect interpretation of Kautsky's thesis that was popularised on the Marxist left can be summarised in the following premises:

    First: Proletarian consciousness is subordinate to the dominant ideology because the proletariat occupies a subordinate position in capitalist society.

236   *Second*: There are emancipators of the proletariat – certain intellectuals

– who possess Marxist theory.

Third: It will be this imported theory and not the action of the proletariat itself that will allow it to break with bourgeois influence and acquire class consciousness.

237   What this way of presenting things undervalues, not to say ignores, is the role played by political practice in developing consciousness.

Do workers set themselves free or must they be set free by others?

238   Kautsky's thesis, thus popularised, directly contradicts Marx's concept of the role played by social practice in the development of consciousness and one of his central theses that the emancipation of the working class should be the work of the working class itself.

239   Marx saw that that economic struggle unified the class.[133] He stressed that it is only through the process of experimentation undertaken by the masses that the move is made from the economic to the political through *circumstances and people themselves being changed simultaneously*. It is in revolutionary practice that this process of the development of consciousness becomes entrenched. And it is through this that *the class in itself becomes the class for itself.*[134]

240   Engels confirms this idea – in a reference to the American working class – when he says that what is important is not so much to import theory into the class, as some German socialists living in the USA wanted to do, but to 'help the working class to begin to move as a class', because once that happened 'they will soon find the right direction'. First, it is important to unite the masses on a national scale: 'anything that might delay or prevent that national consolidation of the working men's party – no matter what platform' would be a mistake.[135]

241   In this sense I find criticism by Marx and Engels of those of their contemporaries who set more store by possessing scientific knowledge than by the practical experience of the masses extremely interesting: they are criticising those who, because of this belief, claimed that parliamentary seats should be in the hands of people who have the time to familiarise themselves with the issues, something workers don't have the opportunity to do. As Marx and Engels say: 'Elect the bourgeoisie then! And later on they say: 'Hence we cannot co-operate with men who say openly that the workers are too uneducated to emancipate themselves

and must first be emancipated from above by philanthropic members of the upper and lower middle classes.'[136]

Experience of struggle enables people to free themselves from the influence of the ruling ideology

242   It is their situation as an exploited class and the bosses' interest in maintaining this situation that sets the working class, as it fights for its immediate needs, on a collision course with those interests. This establishes firstly a difference and then an opposition between working-class interests and ruling-class interests; their fight is no longer a simple economic fight to improve their working conditions or to sell their labour power, it acquires an increasingly political character. They begin questioning isolated features of the capitalist regime, but then become convinced their problems cannot be resolved inside this system and they must fight to build a society governed by a different logic. From this increasingly complex practical experience, there emerges 'a growing consciousness, an ideology of its own which is no longer inscribed on the ideology of the ruling class'.[137]

243   All of this agrees with Marx's conception of the transformation of the 'class in itself' into the 'class for itself', a transformation that leads to the emergence of a world view distinct from that of the bourgeoisie, to the consciousness of being a different class.

244   To say that the working class can acquire class consciousness through its participation in class struggle doesn't mean, however, to ignore that its spontaneous consciousness is very much influenced by the ideas and values of the ruling classes as transmitted through the various facets of the state ideological apparatus. Today, these ideas and values are transmitted mainly by the mass media monopolised by transnational consortia.

245   In normal times, calm times, it would seem that workers could not escape this negative influence and the manipulation of consciousness that is carried out through all these instruments: it is as if invisible nets hold them in a trap from which they cannot escape unless there is a storm.

246   This explains why it is precisely at the beginning of periods of struggle that this confrontation allows workers to discover that laws work in favour of the factory owners and that the police are there to protect not the common good but the interests of the bosses. All of that enables them to become increasingly aware of the antagonism between their interests

as workers and those of the company owners. Their understanding grows – the understanding that the whole institutional system works to the benefit of the aforementioned gentlemen.

247　This is *the living political school*, the school *in the struggle and for the struggle* that Rosa Luxemburg speaks about.[138] She doesn't deny that the proletariat needs a high level of political education, class consciousness and organisation, but maintains that it learns all this not merely from leaflets or pamphlets but in the struggle.

248　Besides, this practical experience doesn't only help to clarify the workers' minds, their way of seeing the world, but also transforms them inwardly, creating in them the feeling that united with other workers they can become a force that can gain victories over the bosses, that they can conquer things. In the struggle, they acquire self-esteem, they feel increasingly capable of achieving their objectives, transforming themselves more and more into the subjects of the process they are a part of.

249　As Michael Lebowitz says, Marx understood very well 'that people are not static, that the struggle for material needs can produce new people with new, "radical" needs'. That is where his thesis about the self-development of the working class through its struggles comes from. And 'even though the needs that they attempt to satisfy do not in themselves go beyond capital, the very process of struggle is one of producing new people, of transforming them into people with a new conception of themselves – as subjects capable of altering their world'.[139]

250　Experience itself is a 'dimension that cannot be replaced because only through it are the subjects of the transformation process created. For these subjects to be created, the masses must educate themselves during their experience of struggle.'[140]

251　And this practical experience makes the workers ask more and more questions, feel a greater desire to understand and to know, creates the necessity to acquire an increasingly profound knowledge of the reality in which they are immersed and of possible solutions to their problems. For that reason it is very different teaching Marxism academically in the universities from teaching it to workers immersed in struggle. For university students it is usually just more knowledge; for workers, a weapon for the struggle.

252　From all that has been said, we can conclude that class consciousness doesn't, therefore, begin just like that when 'science [scientific socialism] is imported', that class consciousness arises in the struggle, and that it is the transformation produced by that struggle and not necessarily the assimilation of a science of history that changes bourgeois consciousness into proletarian consciousness. What Marxist theory does is to enable working-class consciousness to move up to a higher level, as demanded by the class struggle itself. We must not identify class consciousness with the scientific theory of socialism.

253   Marxist theory helps workers to move from the understanding that capital is *unfair* to the recognition that it is *the workers' own product*. This, Marx stressed, is 'an enormous advance in awareness' and 'as much the knell to its [capital's] doom ... as the slave's awareness that he cannot be the property of another'. Marxist theory only helps to empower that consciousness.[141]

254   And that is how Marx explains things when he argues that the strength of the working class is in its numbers, but *numbers weigh in the balance only if united by combination and led by knowledge*. Being many is not enough nor is scientific knowledge enough. If the workers are not able to engage in a unitary practice they will not succeed in throwing off capital's yoke.

255   And capital understands this better than anyone, for one of its strategies is to divide workers in as many ways as possible.

Three levels of consciousness

256   I find it necessary, therefore, to distinguish three levels of consciousness in the working class:

257   *Spontaneous or naïve consciousness* is consciousness necessarily deformed by the effects of the ruling ideology, and most of Althusser's reflections on ideology as deformed knowledge of reality are applicable to this type of consciousness. It is typical, as Sánchez Vázquez says, of a class society in the past, when the working class knew only of *economic* class practice.[142]

258   *Class consciousness* – the very existence of which implies a distancing from bourgeois ideology – is no longer a factor of cohesion for the dominant system but one of antagonism and is not necessarily deformed.[143] This is the consciousness acquired when the class struggle takes on a political dimension, but this consciousness is still not socialist, in as far as it represents resistance to the situation of exploitation rather than a proposal for an alternative to do away with it.

259   *Enlightened class consciousness or socialist consciousness* is that class

consciousness enlightened by Marxist science. All the work Marx put into writing *Capital* was intended to provide workers with the theoretical instruments for their liberation; with the knowledge that enables them not only to react as an exploited class, but also to understand the deep-seated mechanisms of capitalist exploitation and to put forward a new project for an alternative society.

260   Even Rosa Luxemburg, who puts so much emphasis on the fact that class consciousness is acquired through struggle, still recognises the importance of Marxist theory or *socialist theory*, as she calls it, for the labour movement. Writing about the superiority of German social-democratic unions compared to bourgeois and denominational unions, she argues that the material successes and power of the former are the result of *union practice* illuminated by the *theory of scientific socialism*. Without the latter the movement would fall from its height to the level of unsteady groping and mere dull empiricism. 'The strength of the "political practice" of the German unions lies in their insight into the deeper social and economic connections of the capitalist system; but they owe this insight entirely to the theory of scientific socialism upon which their practice is based.'[144]

261   To conclude, I think that it is correct to say that *socialism, as scientific theory, cannot arise solely from the practice of the labour movement but needs to be imported from without.*[145] On the other hand, I think that the acquisition of class consciousness is indeed linked to social practice, to the class struggle. And, of course, the more firmly based it is on socialism as science, the stronger and more coherent it will be.

How this is reflected in the conception of the revolutionary party

262   There is no doubt that the idea that the proletariat must be given Marxist theory from without if it is to liberate itself from spontaneous bourgeois consciousness and acquire proletarian class consciousness has political consequences: consequences that affect both the party as a political instrument and its political practice. Most parties with Leninist roots have suffered from these consequences, although there are always some honourable exceptions.

The leadership: the owners of knowledge

263　It often happens that these parties and, more often, their leading echelons consider themselves to be the bearers of knowledge or of socialist consciousness. They think that the top leadership are the only people capable of formulating the strategy and tactics that must be applied in a disciplined way by the party. This gives rise to a series of deviations, some of which we have mentioned earlier: authoritarianism, verticalism, manipulation of members and the separation of the party from the masses.

264　　If theory is considered to be the property of one group, concrete analyses go by the board. They become redundant, since they are only the *application* of a higher truth. Besides, since ideas come down from above in their definitive form, rank-and-file members can only discuss these ideas in a limited fashion and are not encouraged to come up with any of their own. This is especially the case in a party organised in what Althusser has referred to as *columns*, that is, vertical structures which go from the nuclei or cells up to the political bureau, passing through intermediate bodies. In such an organisation, *any relation between members who belong to different branches, sections or 'columns' is labelled as factional behaviour.*[146]

265　　Analysing what happened in the French Communist Party in 1978 Althusser wrote: 'freedom of discussion at the base had already been won before the Twenty-Second Congress but that in no way changed what the leadership did. This was because the apparatus made the discovery, as old as the bourgeois world, that it could allow itself the luxury of letting members discuss things freely in their cells, with no exceptions nor sanctions, because this would have no results whatsoever. In fact, the real discussions and secret decisions always take place outside of the federations, in the political bureau and the secretariat, or rather, in a small group which doesn't appear in the by-laws. It includes the secretariat, some of the political bureau and some 'experts' or collaborators from the central committee. This is where real decision making takes place.'[147]

The main task: introducing theory into the workers' movement

266　If the most important thing is to get Marxist theory to the workers' movement so that it can acquire class consciousness and liberate itself from bourgeois ideology, then the most important political task for the party will be to bring this fusion about. The party has a tendency to think that it alone possesses the truth, that the masses are backward and must be liberated from the influence of ruling bourgeois ideology by having socialist theory, which they don't possess, bestowed upon them from outside.

Giving priority to education over action

267   The party will give priority to political education over action. It will go to the social movements to identify the most advanced cadres to 'capture' them for the party and educate them there. Care will be taken in the cadre schools to produce educational materials.[148] It is highly improbable that real contact will be made with people, because the top cadres will spend all their time wanting to control people and will always try to replace them.

Uncritical militants

268   The result of an organisation like this is a totally docile, personality-less party member. Since the Party — that is to say, the leadership — is always right, members will tend to voice their complete and uncritical loyalty to the leadership who, for them, embody the party's unity and will.[149]

Chapter 8
Politics as the Art of Making
the Impossible Possible

Is it possible to come up with an alternative?

269   Does accepting that there is a theoretical, organic, programmatic crisis mean we must sit back and do nothing? Can the Left come up with an alternative in spite of being in this situation and the immensely unfavourable correlation of forces in the world?

270   Naturally, the ruling ideology takes it upon itself to say that there is no alternative,[150] but hegemonic groups don't stop at words, they do everything possible to eliminate any alternative that crosses their path. This is what happened to the Popular Unity Front in Chile and the Sandinista revolution in Nicaragua, and it's what they've spent over forty years trying to do to the Cuban revolution[151] and are now doing against the Bolivarian revolution in Venezuela and the revolutionary process that is beginning in Bolivia.

271   Unfortunately, some sectors of the Latin American Left use the argument that politics is *the art of the possible*. When they realise that it is not possible to change things immediately because of the unfavourable correlation of forces that exists today, they think that they have no option but to be realists and accept this impossibility by opportunistically adapting themselves to the existing situation. Looking at politics this way, in fact, excludes any effort to come up with an alternative to capitalism in its present form, because limiting oneself to *realpolitik's* guidelines means being resigned to doing nothing about the existing situation, renouncing one's own politics and submitting oneself to the politics of the ruling classes.

Politics cannot be defined as the art of the possible

272 The Left, if that's what it wants to be, cannot define politics as the art of the possible. *Realpolitik* must be opposed by a notion of politics which is realistic, doesn't deny what is happening but does set about preparing the way to transform existing reality.

273   Gramsci criticised 'excessive' political realism, because this leads to the position that politicians should 'operate only in the sphere of effective reality', and should not concern themselves with 'what should be' but only with what 'is'. This implies that politicians are not capable of seeing beyond their noses. In his opinion, diplomats – not politicians – are those who must move 'solely in effective reality because their particular activity is not to create new equilibria,[152] but, within certain legal limits, to preserve the existing equilibrium'. He thought that a true politician was like Machiavelli: 'a party man, a man with strong passions, a politician of action who wants to create new balances of power, and for that reason can't stop being concerned about what "should be" – not, by the way, to be understood in a moral sense'.

274   But this politician doesn't create from nothing – he starts from effective reality. He dedicates his efforts 'to the creation of a new correlation of forces' using whatever 'is progressive in that reality and strengthening it'. He always '*moves in the plane of effective reality, but so he can control and overcome it (or contribute to it)*'.[153]

275   For the Left, politics must therefore be the art of discovering the potential that exists in the present concrete situation in order to make possible tomorrow that which appears impossible today. A correlation of forces favourable to a popular movement must be built, using that which, its weaknesses notwithstanding, constitutes its strengths.

276   Let's think, for example, about the workers in Marx's time, subjected to the immense power of their capitalist bosses who could, at the drop of a hat, throw them out into the street without any means of survival. Struggle under these conditions was suicide. What then was to be done? Accept exploitation, submitting meekly to it, because it was, at that point, impossible to win the battle? Or fight to change the situation, using the possibilities inherent in their condition as exploited workers: the existence of large concentrations of workers, their ability to organise, and

their identity as an oppressed class? The workers' greatest strength – they were much more numerous than their class enemy – lay in their organisation and unity. However, that strength had to be built and it was only because they followed this path that what initially seemed impossible became possible.

277   Let's use a contemporary example. There's no doubt that today in Latin America the working class's negotiating power has diminished greatly. This is due both to the spectre of lay-offs – those who have a stable wage-paying job are a privileged few – and to the fragmentation that this class has suffered under neo-liberalism. Looking at these objective facts, some claim it is impossible to fight back under these conditions. It is obvious that the classic tactic of union struggle, the strike – which is based on the unity of the industrial working class and its ability to bring production to a halt – is not effective most of the time nowadays. Opportunists, therefore, take advantage of this to try to immobilise the workers' movement and convince it that it should passively accept its existing conditions of over-exploitation. But the art of politics, in contrast, consists in discovering how the present weaknesses – and they really are weaknesses – of the industrial working class can be overcome in order to build a trade union as a social force adapted to the new world situation. *A new union strategy must be built*: nineteenth-century class solidarity is no longer enough. If industrial working-class unity was essential back then, today *the unity of all of those exploited by capital* is essential – permanent and temporary employees, contract workers and those doing outsourced work, *and all other social sectors that have been harmed by the neo-liberal system.*[154]

278   I agree with Isabel Rauber that 'we must formulate a proposal that puts the emphasis back on the central, organizing role of the working class, yet recognises its present weakness and aims to rebuild its strength by encouraging all those who have jobs and the underemployed, unemployed, or marginalized to work together with all those who are oppressed and excluded to build a social force able to go up against the ruling powers with its own power, fight them for power and win'.[155]

279   This is the only way to recover the negotiating power which the working class on its own no longer has, and the rest of the population even more conspicuously lacks.

280   This solution has already been tested in practice. Argentinean unions were successful precisely when they managed to integrate broad sectors

of the population into their movement, as unions in Rio Turbio, Santa Cruz province did.[156]

281   'The only reserves, the only guarantee that unions today can withstand a struggle is by seeking the backing of the rest of the people,' says Alfonso Coñoecar, from Rio Turbio miners' union. 'Today no union can win a battle alone, because neo-liberalism attacks from all sides.'[157]

282   Argentinean labour leader Nestor Piccone, a member of the Congreso de los Trabajadores de Argentina, CTA (Argentinean Workers' Congress) believes that 'representing workers today means recognising their atomisation and the need for coordination. We need a union movement that serves the new class composition. Each stage of history has yielded – from the appropriation of the means of production on – different forms of organisation and representation. Organisations arise out of the demands of certain social sectors, and the New Union Movement must be an expression of those sectors'.[158]

283   This has also been the experience of the Landless Workers' Movement in Brazil (the MST). When the movement worked only with peasants, it was isolated and weak. However, its support began to increase when it understood clearly that it had to change its approach, that it had to concern itself with the problems of other oppressed sectors too (the homeless and the unemployed, for example), and that it was necessary to make urban dwellers understand that the fight for land was not just the battle of a few peasants but also meant a solution for many urgent problems in the city itself. Today it has become the most important point of reference for all social struggles in Brazil and the vanguard of the fight against neo-liberalism.

284   Let's go back to the concept of politics we mentioned earlier. Let us assume that politics is the art of building a national and international social and political force which allows us to change the existing correlation of forces so we can make possible tomorrow what appears impossible at the present. How would this affect the future of those Latin American governments that are involved in a dispute between forces which really want to change society and forces which believe there is no alternative but to submit to the demands of international finance capital? Will that future not depend to a large degree on the capacity of the popular movement to organise, grow and transform itself into a decisive pressure group which will tip the balance towards progressive forces?

Only thus can the programmatic commitment acquired by the presidents in these countries go forward.

285 Left-wing or progressive Latin American leaders should understand – as I believe President Chávez has indeed understood – that they need an organised, politicised people capable of exerting pressure to move the process forward and of fighting against the errors and deviations that arise along the way. They have to understand that our peoples have to be leading, not supporting, actors.

Utopian goals: a source of inspiration

286 A question comes to mind: 'Are there not impossible things which no human action can make possible?' Of course there are. Hinkelammert has called them transcendental impossibilities[159] or utopian goals. These are goals which cannot be achieved, even if all humanity were in agreement. They are desirable goals that contain human values in their pure, definitive form, but which, because of their very perfection, are beyond the reach of human beings, although they do serve to light the way. We are thinking, for example, of Marx's kingdom of equality.

287 The art of politics is also knowing how to discern which of the impossible things are transcendental impossibilities, and which can be made possible if the necessary conditions are created. In this sense, 'utopia becomes a source of inspiration for political realism, a reference for judgment, a reflection on meaning'.[160]

Changing the traditional vision of politics

288 To think about building strength and about the correlation of forces is to *change the traditional view of politics*, which tends to reduce politics to the struggle related to legal and political institutions and exaggerates the role of the state. One immediately thinks of political parties and of the battle 'to direct and control formal instruments of power'.[161] According to this notion of politics, the most radical sectors focus all their political action on *seizing political power and destroying the state*, and the most reformist sectors focus on *administering the political and executive power of government* as the most important (and virtually the sole) form of political practice. The people and their struggles are the great ignored. This is what Helio

Gallardo calls the 'politicism' of the Latin American Left.[162]

289   Some have argued, and rightly so, that the cult of the institution has been the 'Trojan horse' that the ruling system introduced into 'the heart of the transforming Left's fortress';[163] thus managing to undermine the Left from inside.

290   The work of activists has been progressively delegated to people who hold public and administrative positions. *The high-priority effort stopped being collective action and became parliamentary action or obtaining a presence in the media.* The activity of members tended to be reduced to election day, to putting up posters and participating only in isolated and occasional public actions.

291   Worse still, party financing comes increasingly from the participation of party cadres in state institutions, parliament, local government, election boards and the rest, with all that this entails in terms of dependence and vulnerability to pressure.

Overcoming the narrow definition of power

292   To think about building strength is also to look beyond the narrow view which sees power only in the repressive aspects of the state. The enemy's power is not only repressive, says Carlos Ruiz, 'it also builds, moulds, disciplines ... if the power of the ruling classes acted only to censor, to exclude, to impose obstacles and repressive measures, it would be more fragile. If it is stronger it is because, as well as avoiding what it doesn't like, it is capable of creating what it does like, of moulding behaviour, of producing knowledge, rationalities and consciousness, of forging a way of seeing both the world and itself....'[164]

293   To think about building is also to overcome the old, deeply-rooted mistake of trying to build a *political force* – whether through arms or the ballot box – without building a *social force*.[165]

Politics as the art of building a social force in opposition to the system

294   The birth of a social force in opposition to the system – in other words, an anti-capitalist force – is what the ruling classes fear most, and their narrow conception of politics as a struggle to conquer spaces of power in

the institutional legal-political apparatus stems from that fear.

295   For the Left, on the other hand, politics must be the art of constructing a social force in opposition to the system. But this is only possible if it succeeds in 'dismembering the barriers that the enemy puts up to prevent this force being built. This is why it is so important to have a broad understanding of all these barriers and not just to observe them and go up against only some of them. These barriers are precisely the way the ruling classes are wont to organise the dominated, politically and socially.'[166]

296   The Left must not, therefore, see the people or popular social forces as something given that can be manipulated and only needs to be stirred up, but as something that has to be built.[167] It must also see that the ruling classes have a strategy to prevent this from happening. This implies not getting carried away by the situation, but acting on it, choosing in which of the existing spaces and conflicts efforts must be concentrated in order to achieve the principal objective – building the popular force. This building process doesn't happen spontaneously, it needs a subject who builds, a political subject able to direct his or her actions according to an analysis of the overall political dynamic. Obviously this political subject will need first to overcome the errors and deviations described above.

Chapter 9
Why We Need a Political Organisation

297 Because of the twentieth-century Left's errors and deviations, the crisis of politics and politicians we analysed earlier, and the original and combative action of some new social movements and actors, there has been a tendency – which is on the rise – to dismiss political parties and even the slightest move towards centralising the leadership of any struggle. Some suggest that at the current stage in the fight, we can do without parties and the Left's task should be confined to coordinating these groups and minority interests – race, gender, sexual or cultural preferences of any kind – around a common purpose.

298 To back up their arguments they point to the practices of the world movement against globalisation. At the 1999 Seattle protests, for example, 'what most surprised and puzzled observers was that groups previously thought to be in opposition to each other – trade unionists and environmentalists, church groups and anarchists, and so forth – acted together without any central, unifying structure that subordinates or sets aside their differences'.[168]

299 However, it is one thing to manage to hold successful one-off demonstrations against globalisation or the war in Iraq, but something else entirely to succeed in overthrowing a government and using the power gained to build a model of a society that is an alternative to capitalism.

300 I am not against a proposal to coordinate all these social actors, and I do not believe anyone sees it as a negative thing. However, I fully share the British historian Eric Hobsbawm's concern that the sum of these minorities does not a majority make; that if these groups unite only

73

because their immediate interests are the same, that unity 'looks very much like that of states temporarily allied in a war against a common enemy which then disintegrates once their common goal disappears'.[169]

301 The countless individual and collective members of the non-party Left do not have the means to coordinate their many different demands, or to channel and express their discontent in an organised fashion, or to generate spaces of social opposition which progress from being myriad expressions of resistance to constituting a real danger to the system's self-reproduction.

302 And why does this possibility not exist?

303 First, because *transformation doesn't just happen spontaneously*, the ruling ideas and values in capitalist society – that rationalise and justify the existing order – permeate the whole of society and exert their greatest influence on the popular sectors. Second, because it is necessary to formulate a social project that is an alternative to capitalism, a project for a different country. Third, we have to be able to defeat vastly more powerful forces that oppose such a transformation. And defeating them isn't possible without a political body that 'formulates proposals and is capable of giving millions of people a single will'[170] while at the same time unifying and coordinating various emancipatory practices.

The effects of the ruling ideology

304 With regard to the first point, we must remember that 'the view that people have of the world is historically constructed',[171] and that this world view, also known as common sense, is to a lesser or greater degree shaped by the ideological influences of the ruling class – under capitalism this is bourgeois ideology. This is particularly true among those sectors of the population which lack the theoretical weapons to distance themselves critically from this ideology.

Manufacturing consent

305 No one any longer disputes the ability of modern mass media to influence public opinion. The media, which are increasingly concentrated in fewer hands, take it on themselves to 'channel thought and attitudes' within parameters acceptable to the ruling classes and thus deflect 'any potential

challenge to established privilege and authority' before it 'can take form and gather strength'.[172] According to Chomsky, bourgeois liberals set only one condition for accepting the democratic game: that, by controlling the media, they can 'manufacture consent' and 'tame the bewildered herd'.[173]

306   By converting politics into a *marketplace for ideas*, the ruling classes – who have a monopoly on *manufacturing consent* – have the weapons needed to lead the man or woman in the street into parties charged with safeguarding their interests. The free market does not lead to free opinions, although they would have us believe it does. As Benjamin Ginsberg says: 'the hidden hand of the market can be almost as potent an instrument for control as the iron fist of the state';[174] this echoes Chomsky's verdict, quoted earlier, that 'propaganda is to democracy as the bludgeon is to the totalitarian state'.[175]

307   This alone explains why it is the most conservative parties – which defend the interests of an infinitesimal minority of the population – that have transformed themselves, quantitatively speaking, into mass parties[176] and explains why the social base of their support, in Latin America at least, is the poorest sectors of the urban periphery and rural areas.

308   These mechanisms for manufacturing consent are not only used during election campaigns; they begin much earlier, influencing people's daily lives through the family, education, culture and recreation. It has been shown that 'the most effective and long lasting political "indoctrination" is that which takes place outside the political sphere and does not use political language'.[177]

309   This is why these people should be exposed to other experiences and sources of knowledge that help them to change their world view, discover the underlying causes of their exploitation, and, as a result, find their path to liberation.

310   This is not to say that in certain situations the people cannot waken from its slumber and discover the real interests that motivate various social sectors. This is what happens during periods of great social upheaval and revolution. The ruling classes remove their masks and expose their methods of struggle. Peoples become politicised and learn at an astounding rate.[178]

311   The 11 April 2002 military coup in Venezuela against the democratically elected president, Hugo Chávez, allowed the population to see who was who: the pro-coup senior officers in the armed forces were

unmasked; the fascist intentions of many opposition politicians, self-proclaimed democrats, were clearly exposed. The level of political consciousness in the popular sectors increased enormously. The people learned in a few days far more than it could have learned from books in years.

Direct knowledge and indirect knowledge

312   This problem invites us to look at the difference between the *direct knowledge* and the *indirect knowledge* that a social actor may possess. There is a type of knowledge to which workers and the poorer social sectors in general may have access as a result of the confrontations they have been through. That's why it is so important that revolutionaries build upon the historical and social knowledge that has been accumulated by the people: ideas, values, beliefs, forms of organisation and struggle and styles of work. But there is another type of knowledge to which it is not possible for them to gain direct access. It is very difficult for the poorer sectors on their own to acquire a global understanding of the class struggle in their country and in the rest of the world.

313   Marxist organisations have often tended to overvalue this indirect knowledge, a large part of which is derived from academic research, and to undervalue other ways of producing knowledge, such as those based on direct experience, on collective and social practice. There is a tendency to deny the importance of any knowledge the oppressed sectors manage to acquire through direct experience. 'The importance of direct experience for producing knowledge is negated, especially when it's a question of the social experiences of ordinary men and women'.[179] As Carlos Ruiz points out, this leaves the analysis of reality in the hands of intellectuals.

314   It is also true that some have gone to the opposite extreme of greatly overestimating the value of direct experience as the only source of knowledge, scorning the need for an overall, critical view of both the national and international situation.

315   We need to reject two extreme theses: that of the *enlightened vanguard*, and *rank and filism*. The first considers that only the political organisation is capable of knowing the truth: the party is the conscience, the repository of wisdom, the masses a backward sector. The opposite

extreme is rank and filism. This greatly overestimates the potential of social movements. It believes that these movements are self-sufficient. It indiscriminately rejects the intervention of any type of political body and, by doing so, often encourages divisions in the mass movement.

316   In order to give impetus to profound social transformation, an organisation is needed in which 'political analysis is undertaken as a synthesis of a collective knowledge-building process which integrates both direct experience and an assessment of global reality from a theoretical perspective. This can only be orchestrated by a political organisation which is conceived of as an authentic "collective intellectual".'[180]

Drawing up a social project that is an alternative to capitalism

317 A political organisation is necessary, in the second place, because there is a need for a body to design a project that is an alternative to capitalism. We have already seen that this undertaking needs time, research and knowledge of the national and international situation. It is not something that can be improvised overnight, and far less so in the complex world in which we live. And this project must be encapsulated in a programme that is to the organisation what navigation charts are to sailors.

318   The programme allows us to orientate ourselves and not to lose our way; to move forward confidently, not to confuse what has to be done now and what has to be done later, to know what 'steps to take and how to take them'.

319   Many programmes that are very revolutionary on paper can become a brake on the process if people try to use them as a banner for the immediate struggle. Instead of bringing forces together they scare them away.

320   One of the Left's most common mistakes in certain Latin American revolutionary sectors has been the inability to draw up a minimum programme that, following an exhaustive analysis of the concrete reality of the country in question, of the region and of the world, indicates the immediate tasks, tasks that enable the party to mobilise the broadest spectrum of the masses against the main obstacle facing the revolutionary movement at that moment.

The need to give millions of people a single will

321   A political organisation is necessary, in the third place, because we must be capable of overcoming the vastly more powerful forces opposing the transformation for which we're fighting. This will not be possible, as I argued earlier, 'without a body that formulates proposals and is capable of giving millions of people a single will';[181] that is to say, a body that unifies and coordinates the various emancipatory practices around goals common to all actors. When we talk of unifying we are thinking of 'grouping together', 'uniting' the various actors around these goals which are of common interest. Unify by no means implies 'to make uniform', 'to homogenise' nor does it mean to suppress differences but rather to act in common, building on the different characteristics of each group.

322   The anti-globalisation or anti-war movement is *multicoloured*[182] and must continue to be so, but I don't think that is anything new: as Hardt and Negri argue, all victorious revolutions were multicoloured and were victorious precisely because they were able to unite various actors around a single cause. All we have to do is analyse the slogans that led to their victories: peace, bread and freedom in Russia; the battle against the tyrant of the day in Cuba and Nicaragua. Whether the differences between the actors who took part in the struggle were or were not respected afterwards is another thing altogether.

323   The history of the many popular uprisings in the twentieth century has demonstrated overwhelmingly that the creative initiative of the masses is no longer enough to overthrow the ruling regime. What happened in May 1968 in France is one of the many examples that corroborate this assertion. Other cases closer both in time and in space are the various popular uprisings that took place in Haiti in 1987 and 1988, the social explosions that shook Venezuela and Argentina in the 1990s when the impoverished urban masses, with no defined leadership, rose up, seized highways and towns and looted food shops. In spite of their size and combativeness, these movements did not succeed in destroying the ruling system.

324   The history of triumphant revolutions, on the other hand, demonstrates over and over again what can be achieved when there is a political body which is capable, first, of advancing a national alternative programme

which acts as a glue for the most disparate popular sectors and, second, is capable of concentrating their strength on the decisive link, in other words, the weakest link in the enemy's chain.

325   This political body is, as Trotsky said, the piston that compresses the steam at the crucial moment, making sure it doesn't dissipate but is converted into the locomotive's driving force.

326   If political action is to be effective, and the popular movement's acts of protest, resistance and struggle are to achieve their anti-system goals, there needs to be an organising subject capable of directing and unifying the multiple initiatives that arise spontaneously and capable of encouraging more initiatives.

327   Solid organisational cohesion doesn't only produce the objective capacity to act; it also creates an internal climate that enables the organisation to make an energetic intervention in important events and to make good use of the opportunities arising therefrom. It is important to remember that in politics it's necessary not only to be right, but also *to be right at the right time*, and to have the forces needed to put one's ideas into practice.

328   If this is not the case, a feeling of not having a solid organisation and the insecurity caused by not being able to implement decisions because of a lack of discipline have a negative influence that can be paralysing.

329   I have no doubt that many of those who are unwilling to discuss the need for political instruments identify these instruments with the anti-democratic, authoritarian, bureaucratic, homogenising single party, which they rightly reject. I believe that it is very important to overcome this subjective block because I am convinced, as I wrote earlier, that there can be no effective struggle against the current system of domination, nor can an alternative socialist society be built, without the existence of a body capable of bringing all the actors together and of unifying their will for action around the goals they set.

330   It is paradoxical that Hardt and Negri – who admit that we live in a 'global state of war',[183] while the full democracy we want has yet to be built, who justify the use of violence as self-defence against imperial power, who say that the multitude, 'is a project of political organization and thus can be achieved only through political practices'[184] and that 'the multitude must be able to make decisions and act in common'[185] – do not accept the idea that there should be a 'central point of command and

intelligence'[186] and have no suggestions whatsoever on how to implement the decisions taken by common action.

331   Since I agree with these authors that 'if the Left is to be resurrected and reformed it will only be done on the basis of new practices, new forms of organization, and new concepts',[187] I shall now explain my vision of the new political instrument that the new times need.

332   I have absolutely no doubt that to be able to put these ideas into practice we must find new forms of political expression, either by rejuvenating existing parties, wherever possible, or by creating new political instruments.

333   Since to 'politicise' does not mean to 'party-ise' but means transforming those who are suffering from injustice and oppression into subjects who are resolved to do their part to change this situation, we do not necessarily have to think about the traditional formula for a Left *party* when we think about the need to build a *political instrument*.

PART III
The New Political Instrument

Chapter 10
The Characteristics of the New Political Instrument

Understanding the importance of social practice for creating consciousness

334   If we start out from the thesis that the working class and the popular movement can only liberate themselves through the struggles they engage in, then the new or renewed political organisation must be compatible with this thesis. This implies a profound change in the way of thinking about politics and the organisation.

335   Politics cannot be reduced to political institutions, and the role of the state must not be exaggerated. The narrow view of power – as we have said before – which thinks power resides only in the repressive state apparatus must be discarded. We have to understand that a political force cannot be built without building a social force.

336   Instead of placing so much importance on importing theory into the workers' movement, the new political organisation should pay close attention to the various ways social discontent with the oppressive ruling system is manifested and to the initiatives and kinds of struggle that arise from these forms of discontent. It should also create spaces where those social sectors and grassroots initiatives which feel themselves to be affected by the existing situation can meet. Working in conjunction with the social movement, it should try to discover the spaces and ways of confrontation that allow this movement to become increasingly aware that it will only overcome its ills when all unite and build a social force capable of going up against the existing system of class domination.

An organisation immersed in society

337 The new political organisation must be deeply involved in society, immersed in the popular sectors. The strength of the organisation should be assessed not so much by the number of members it has or by the internal activities that the party puts on, but by the influence that it has in society.

338 As Enrique Rubio says, 'it's not about putting people in the party organisation or society into the party's project but rather about putting politics into people's lives and the party organisation into society'.[188] Member identity ought to be legitimised by what is done *outside* not *inside* the party. This means that members of the new organisation should occupy most of their time in forging links between the party and society.[2] Intra-party activities should be reduced to what is strictly necessary and a culture of excessive meetings should be avoided. Intra-party activities that I think are of great importance are those to do with the political education of members, activities that many Left organisations today have put on the back burner with results damaging to their future. They end up with no trained cadres, who can take over from older cadres, who did indeed receive a systematic political education.

Overcoming the tendency to homogenise

339 The party Left still finds it difficult to work with difference. The tendency, especially in class parties, was always to homogenise the social base where they did their work. If this could be justified in the past because of the identity and homogeneity of the working class among whom these parties did most of their work, it is an anachronism now because there is such a wide range of social actors. Today it's more a question of unity in diversity, of respect for ethnic, cultural and gender differences and of a sense of belonging to specific collectives. This makes it necessary to attempt to channel members' commitments according to the potential of each sector or person, without trying to homogenise the actors. This is where the idea comes from that groups that are already working together because they have similar interests and activities can develop their activism using those same groups as a base. It is important to have a special sensitivity to be able to perceive all points of contact that

could enable the organisation, mindful of the differences, to advance a platform of common struggle.

New times, new language

340   This respect for difference must also be reflected in the language used. It is essential to break with the old style of trying to send the same message to people who may have very different interests. One cannot go around imagining amorphous masses; what exist are individuals, men and women who are in different places, doing different things and subject to different ideological influences. The message must become flexible if it is to reach this concrete individual. We must be capable of *tailoring the message to the individual*.

341   The Left's messages in the television age cannot be the same as they were in the 1960s or in Gutenberg's time either.[190] We are living in the era of the image, of the soap opera. 'The culture of the book, of the written word', as Atilio Borón says, 'is an élite culture today; it is no longer a mass culture.'[191] People today read very little or not at all. To communicate with them we have to master audiovisual language. And the Left faces a big challenge: how to do this when the major audiovisual media are completely controlled by huge national and transnational monopolies.

342   There is often a desire to compete with the major television channels, but this is clearly impossible. Not only are the financial resources lacking but, even when an organisation has the money, the economic groups that monopolise the media don't let the Left enter the market.

343   There are, however, alternative forms of communication in Latin America that the Left hasn't yet explored enough; these include community radio, neighbourhood newspapers and municipal television channels. And there is something even more accessible to any group that does community work: the use of VCRs and DVDs to show to small groups of people experiences that might interest them. This allows them to learn and to develop a critical consciousness concerning the messages and information broadcast by huge transnational media corporations.

344   We are therefore faced with the challenge of creating educational videos that enable social movements to share experiences and learn from one another.

345   People's radio stations linked into networks and broadcast by satellite have started to play an important role in experience sharing. They allow social actors to communicate amongst themselves and between countries and talk about their experiences.

Overcoming hegemonism

346   The Left must give up all vestiges of a hegemonist attitude if it is to be capable of coordinating all the forces opposed to neo-liberalism.

347   I should make it clear that hegemonism must not be confused with *hegemony*. The latter is *the opposite of hegemonism*. It has nothing to do with the steamroller policy that some revolutionary organisations, availing themselves of the fact that they are the strongest, have tried to use to get others to support their policies. Nor does it have anything to do with the attitude of trying to charge royalties to organisations that dare to fight for the same causes.

348   If a group is to exercise hegemony, others must accept as their own the proposals that this group, political front or movement puts forward.

349   It is not a question of manipulating but, on the contrary, of rallying all those who are convinced and attracted by the project to be undertaken. And people will only join an undertaking where there is respect for others, where responsibilities are shared with other forces.

350   Of course, this is easier said than done. What tends to happen is that when one organisation is strong, it often undervalues the support that other organisations can give. This is something that has to be fought against.

351   Instead of bringing in new support, a hegemonist attitude has the opposite effect. On the one hand, it creates discontent in other Left organisations; they feel manipulated and obliged to accept decisions in which they have not taken any part. On the other hand, it reduces the number of potential allies since an organisation which assumes this type of position is incapable of representing the real interests of all the popular sectors and makes many of them sceptical and distrustful.

352   Moreover, the concept of hegemony is a dynamic one. Hegemony is not achieved once and for all. *A constant process of renewal* is necessary to keep it. Life goes on, new problems appear and, with them, new challenges. If the organisation is not capable of responding to these, it could lose its influence in society.

353   Today, important sectors of the Left have come to understand that it will have greater hegemony when it manages to get more people to follow its political line, even if this does not happen under its banner. And the best way to do this is to win as much support for these ideas as possible, support not only from political and grassroots organisations and their natural leaders but also from important figures in national life.

354   The degree of hegemony achieved cannot, therefore, be measured by the number of office holders a party has. What is crucial is that those who are in office adopt the line of the political organisation as their own and implement it, even if they are not members of that organisation. Moreover, if a party does have many of its members holding office in a given organisation, great care must be taken not to fall into hegemonist deviations. It is easier for those holding such a position to impose their ideas on others than to risk the challenge that winning people over implies.

Creating a new relationship with the popular movement

Respecting its autonomous development

355   If we think that practical struggle is of the utmost importance if the people's consciousness is to develop, our political instrument must show great respect for popular movements. It must contribute to their autonomous development, leaving all attempts at manipulation behind. Its basic premise must be that political cadres aren't the only people who have ideas and suggestions; on the contrary, popular movements have a lot to offer because through their daily struggles they learn, discover new ways, find answers, and invent methods which can be very useful.

356   If there is anything sabotaging the relationship of the party Left with popular movements – and with the new social actors in general – it is the authoritarian style of most of their cadres, who are used to leading the masses by giving them orders. Yet social movements, and especially the new actors, don't take kindly to being led; they need to be convinced, to give their support freely and consciously to proposals that arise from outside their own movements.

357   New actors are particularly sensitive about the subject of democracy. Their struggles have generally begun by fighting back against oppression and discrimination. Small wonder, therefore, that they don't want to be

manipulated; instead they demand that their autonomy be respected and that they be allowed to participate democratically in the decision-making process. They promote consensus in their own organisations, and, if that is unattainable, they believe that decisions must be adopted by a very large majority. 'They avoid using narrow majorities to impose their will on the minority. They believe that if most people are unconvinced, it makes no sense to impose a measure adopted by a narrow majority. In their opinion, it is preferable to wait until people mature and come to see the merits of a given measure by themselves.... This approach prevents the damaging internal divisions that often plague Left movements and parties and avoids really serious mistakes.'[192]

358   As Clodomiro Almeyda said, *creative, new, revolutionary, transforming ideas* do not have to originate only within the party – so the party, therefore, need not limit itself to collecting demands that originate within the movement. It should also collect ideas and concepts that enrich its own conceptual arsenal.[193] The relationship with popular movements then, should be a *two-way street*. Unfortunately, it still tends be a one-way street.

359   Moreover, coordinating the party Left with the social Left would be easier if the traditional narrow conception of politics were discarded; this tends to reduce politics to the struggle that has to do with political-legal institutions and to exaggerate the role of the state.[194] This conception permeates both the most radical and the most reformist sectors. We have seen that politics is reduced by the former to taking power and destroying the state, and by the latter to administering political power or running the government. For both, the people and their struggles are the great ignored.

The people's motives are the starting point

360   It must also be understood that it is a huge mistake to try to lead grassroots movements by ordering them around, by coming to them with already-worked-out plans. The political instrument's role is to facilitate, not to supersede. We have to fight to eliminate any sign of verticalism, which cancels out people's initiative: popular participation is not something that can be decreed from above. Only by working with people's motives, only if they are helped to work out for themselves why certain tasks are necessary, and only when we win over their hearts and minds will they be willing to commit themselves fully to the actions they undertake.

361   Wherever possible, we must include the rank and file in the decision-making process and this means creating spaces where people can express their opinions.

Learning to listen

362   This means that we must learn to listen, to speak to people and then, from all the thoughts that have been collected, we must be able to make the right diagnosis of the people's mood; be able to synthesise anything that can unite them and generate action; be able to fight against any pessimistic, defeatist thinking that exists. We must listen carefully to all solutions the people themselves come up with for defending themselves or for fighting for their demands.

363   Only then will the instructions given not be seen as orders coming from outside the movement. They will, instead, help to build an organisational process capable of encouraging, if not all, at least many of the people to join the struggle. Then, building on that, it will be possible gradually to win over the more backward and pessimistic sectors. When the latter understand that the aims being fought for are not only necessary but possible, they too – as Che said – will join in the struggle.

Make sure the people feel they are the active subjects

364   Besides, when the people realise that it is their ideas and initiatives that are being put into practice, they will feel that they are the active subjects of what happens, they will grow as human beings and their willingness to struggle will increase exponentially.

Moving from military-style leadership to popular education methods

365   After all that has been said up to this point we can understand that political cadres for the new era cannot be cadres with a military mentality – today we are not leading an army, which is not to say that at some critical junctures, there might not be a need for such a shift. Nor can they be populist demagogues, because we are not leading a flock of sheep. Political cadres should be, basically, *popular educators*, capable of empowering all the wisdom existing among the people – that derived from their cultural traditions and their tradition of struggle as well as that acquired in their daily battle for survival – by merging it with the most

comprehensive knowledge that the political organisation can contribute. Creative initiative and the search for answers must be encouraged.

366   Unfortunately, many leaders were educated in a top-down leadership style and that is not easy to change overnight. I do not, therefore, want to encourage excessive optimism. We still have a long way to go to find a solution to the problem of the correct relationship with popular movements.

367   I agree with Adolfo Gilly that unless the relationship between the political organisation and social movements is established 'on participatory and not subordinate terms, then ... the dangers of co-optation, bureaucratisation, and conservatism are very great. Elitism in politics is not a deformation but one of the implications, one of the possible consequences when citizen participation decreases or doesn't find the channels and means through which to express itself.'[195]

368   This reassessment of social movements and the understanding that leadership is something earned and not imposed have prompted some sectors of the Left to seek new formulas for forming political fronts which are not simply alliances between political parties, but spaces where social movements can express themselves.

No more workerism

369   If the new political organisation's theory is based on a correct assessment of social practice, it must take into account not only the economic exploitation of the workers, but also all the other kinds of oppression – the destruction of humanity and nature that cannot be explained simply by the relationship between capital and labour.

370   It must abandon class reductionism by taking responsibility for defending all social groups that are excluded and discriminated against economically, socially, politically and culturally. While it should be concerned with class problems, its concern must also extend to ethno-cultural, race, gender, class, sex, and environmental problems. It must bear in mind not only organised workers' struggles but also the struggles of women, First Nations people, people of African descent, young people, children, retired people, the differently abled, gays, etcetera.[196]

371   It is a question of no longer simply taking responsibility for defending all those exploited and discriminated against, but also of understanding

'the radical political and transformative potential that exists in the struggles' waged by all these sectors.[197]

372   Since ecological movements tackle a problem that affects all of humanity – the deterioration of the environment – I agree with Helio Gallardo that this movement 'could act as a catalyst and a coordinating axis along which other struggles can join in shaping an alternative sensibility for change';[198] more recently, the anti-war movement in the more developed countries has brought about a very broad-based convergence.

A body to coordinate all the different emancipatory social practices

373   The new political organisation should not try to gather to its bosom all the legitimate representatives of struggles for emancipation but should strive to coordinate their practices into a single political project,[199] by generating – as Helio Gallardo says – '*meeting spaces* so that the assorted social groups and their discontents can recognise each other and grow' in consciousness and in the specific struggle that each one has to wage in its own area: the neighbourhood, university, school, factory, etcetera.[200]

374   Gallardo argues that 'a constructive tension between social movements should arise; they should not lose their autonomy and roots, because those are their source of strength; let parties or organic structures of a new kind bring these social movements together, let them not try to represent them nor suffocate them, but most importantly, do let them take on the job of creating a national project.[201] It's very difficult for a social movement – whether of young people, ecologists, women, peasants, people of African descent or indigenous peoples – to be able to come up with a national project.

Democracy: the cause to champion

375   The new political organisation must take democracy as its cause because it understands that the fight for democracy is inseparable from the struggle for socialism.

376   But before continuing, I think it's important to define what I understand by democracy.

377   I believe that a democratic regime must take three central aspects into

consideration: representativity and civil rights, social equality, and political participation by the people as active subjects.

Political or representative democracy

378   The first aspect, *political or representative democracy*, refers basically to the political regime; it focuses on the freedom to elect those who govern and on civil rights for all citizens. This democracy, which proclaims itself to be the people's government, can be – and this is in fact what happens with bourgeois democracy – a democracy that benefits only a minority of the population. This is why it is sometimes referred to as formal or representative democracy since, in the name of the people, it benefits only a minority. It creates first- and second-class citizens. And for that reason it is becoming more and more discredited.

379   Nevertheless, we cannot reject all kinds of representation because of the bad use to which bourgeois democracy has put this concept. Under socialism, there must be a system which allows citizens to be represented. 'It isn't', as Sánchez Vázquez says, 'a matter of advocating the abolition of representative democracy or delegated participation in the name of direct participation, which far from excluding delegated participation complements and enriches it.'[202]

380   One cannot govern without delegating government tasks to representatives of the people. Direct democracy is viable at the local level, in small communities, but it cannot be exercised on the national level, except in exceptional cases (plebiscites, referenda).

381   What must be rejected then, are not the representative aspects of democracy but bourgeois democracy which favours privileged sectors of society and which, therefore has no interest whatsoever in creating mechanisms for direct democracy.

382   Therefore, I think all reflections on the technical aspects of representativity – I call them 'representativity techniques' – are valuable. These seek to ensure real representativity and a system of accountability to the electors. I believe that the Left should make efforts to ensure that all minority currents are represented and protected at the state level – provided, of course, that their interests don't conflict with national interests.

383   It seems to me that the new society should also have instruments to defend itself against the demagoguery of bourgeois electoral campaigns,

in which everything is promised and little or nothing is delivered. Therefore, it should be a basic principle of this kind of representativity that mechanisms are developed that enable the electorate to recall those representatives who have ceased to carry out their mandate.

384   In addition the terms in office granted by the people need to be limited. Setting limits on the length of time someone can be in office avoids the trauma entailed when it becomes necessary to remove a leadership cadre from office – the moral, family, and social trauma. This is traumatic because all dismissals, if they are not provided for in any regulation, are seen as punishment.

Real or social democracy

385   The second variety is known as *real, substantial or social democracy*; its fundamental purpose is to find a solution to the problems that affect people the most: food, land, work, education, housing: all those things that make it possible to move towards a more egalitarian society. In practice, this form of democracy can be exercised by a political system that doesn't function in the traditional manner of Western representative democracy.

Participatory democracy

386   But socialism's identifying characteristic must be the existence of participatory democracy. The people collectively constitute the real active subject who builds the new society where all forms of popular self-organisation are encouraged and respected, with no attempt being made to subject people to the party or the state.

387   As a project, socialism cannot be separated from democracy; it cannot be anything but the highest expression of democracy and must greatly expand democracy in comparison with limited bourgeois democracy.

Democracy can't be decreed into existence, it has to be built

388   After the experience of the recent dictatorships in the southern cone of Our America and of various types of authoritarian governments in many other Latin American countries, the Marxist Left – which didn't sufficiently value democracy because it associated the word 'democracy' with bourgeois representative democracy – understood that it had to rescue the cause of democracy, which until then had been in the hands of centrist and conservative forces. The challenge was to reappropriate

democracy and give it its full meaning – not just its political, but its social and participatory meaning.

389   The defeat suffered by the socialist countries in Eastern Europe and the Soviet Union made the need for this reappropriation even more clear. The alternative, socialist society that we want to build must be completely democratic. What we perhaps do not understand is that democracy cannot be decreed into existence from above, that democracy is not possible if people do not undergo a process of cultural transformation, and that this is achieved not only through political education or ideological propaganda but also through practice. As Marx says, people change their circumstances and change themselves through their practice.

390   It is therefore essential that those of us who fight for an alternative society, who work with popular movements and with Left or progressive governments, understand that we need to create spaces for real participation, both where people work and where they live, and in schools, universities and elsewhere. If people do not become actors, the active subjects of their own history, we shall be able to solve some of our peoples' problems – health, food, education, housing – but we shall not be able to ensure that people transform themselves into the subjects of their own destiny.

391   I think that the reason for the fall of the socialist countries in Eastern Europe and of the USSR had quite a lot to do with this lack of participation. The citizens of those countries were not motivated to defend regimes that turned them into observers rather than actors.

392   We have to fight for a new kind of democracy, built from the bottom up and for those at the bottom, using local governments, rural communities, workers' and citizens' fronts.

Eliminating the expression 'dictatorship of the proletariat'?

393   However, when they rightly champion the cause of democracy, some sectors of the Left have thought it necessary to call into question one of the cornerstones of Marxism: the dictatorship of the proletariat.

394   I think that Marxists have been on the defensive over this. However, when rightly rejecting the term 'dictatorship of the proletariat', what they have also done is to cast aspersions on the core of Marxist thinking about the state.

395   We have to understand that in Marx's opinion this dictatorship was not incompatible with democracy. According to Jon Elster, the 'dictatorship of the proletariat' is 'a phrase that has acquired an ominous sense unknown to Marx and his contemporaries. Dictatorship in his era and his work was not incompatible with democracy.'[203]

396   I think that things must be made very clear so that we can understand each other. I believe that we should cease to use the phrase 'dictatorship of the proletariat'. Words are tools for communication; when one uses a term and no one understands what is being said, or they understand something entirely different from what is intended, then what is the point of using it? Just to give an example, when one talks to people about that liquid people drink, one says 'water', not H_2O; similarly, it makes no sense to use the term 'dictatorship of the proletariat' in political discourse, particularly since in recent decades in Latin America what was seen, what people knew, were military dictatorships. How are we going to tell people who haven't studied Marxism, or who have no theoretical knowledge: 'Friends, we're here to offer you a new dictatorship, only now it's the dictatorship of the proletariat'?

397   Now, political discourse is one thing and theoretical discourse is another. From the theoretical point of view, if a democratic political system is to reflect the interests of the majority of the people, it must necessarily place restrictions on the interests of those who oppose the adoption of measures that benefit the people.

398   Real societies are not castles in the air where everyone has the same interests. It is important to understand that societies are composed of contradictory interests and therefore, in order for a society of popular majorities to function, it will have to employ mechanisms that ensure majority interests are respected. Naturally, this will lead to a conflict with the interests of the minority that has enjoyed all the privileges up until that point. And this minority will only surrender its privileges when pushed. This is the law of history. If the minority would voluntarily submit to the interests of the popular majority in power, then the latter could establish an unlimited democracy. I didn't invent this idea – Lenin himself said it. The limits are not set by the people but by the enemy's behaviour.

399   The dictatorship of the proletariat is only the other side of a broader, popular democracy, in other words, of the right to take steps to ensure

the rights of the majority are respected. If this right were not exercised against an opposition that opposes the very concept of democracy, the majority would not be respected.

400   The concept of dictatorship was developed by Marx, and especially by Lenin in 'The State and Revolution', to explain how the state functions. According to them, even the most representative – that is, most democratic – bourgeois democracies are still bourgeois dictatorships because they are expressions of the supremacy or rule of the bourgeois class, as the interests of that class are imposed on the rest of society. No bourgeois politician, of course, is going to run a political campaign by championing the cause of the dictatorship of the bourgeoisie. On the contrary, they will try to make people believe that their system represents the interests of all citizens and is the most democratic system in the world.

401   The dictatorship of the proletariat does not mean, therefore, not respecting the laws that the people themselves have made or eliminating the rule of law, but rather using this rule of law against the minority who oppose reforms introduced by a democratic decision.

402   Nevertheless we must not confuse 'the rule of law' with the 'rule of the Right'.[204] The bourgeoisie, which passionately advocates the rule of law when it is *their* rule of law, places huge obstacles in the path of progressive and revolutionary forces when they try to modify this rule of law in an effort to introduce constitutional reforms which better embody the people's interests, as is happening today in Venezuela with Chávez.

403   This is why the Marxist distinction between type of state and form of government is so important. The type of state responds to the question: whose interests, (or the interests of which class) does this state serve? The form of government answers a different question: how are those interests served: through a dictatorial regime or through one of the many varieties of democratic regime? It is important to understand that when the classic texts refer to 'the dictatorship of the proletariat' they're thinking about a kind of state and not a form of government. Furthermore, they are thinking about the type of state in a developed capitalist society which is moving towards socialism – a society therefore composed mostly of the bourgeoisie and the proletariat. Thus, one talks of a dictatorship of the bourgeoisie or the dictatorship of the proletariat, with no shades of grey in between.

404   Bearing in mind what has been said up to this point, perhaps the best

way to avoid confusion without renouncing the Marxist concept of state (which maintains that the state is not neutral, but obeys the interests of a certain class) is to refer to a state where the bourgeoisie has hegemony or one where the people have hegemony. This enables us to avoid the misunderstanding inherent in the term 'dictatorship', while allowing us to better reflect the social actors now present in the Latin American revolutionary process, which includes many other social sectors besides the proletariat.

405   This failure to understand the relationship between socialism and democracy was reflected in the language used by many leaders of the Left. They declared themselves to be revolutionaries and labelled other progressive Leftist forces 'democratic forces', as if a radical revolutionary didn't also have to be a radical democrat.

406   Instead of claiming democracy as their own, their speeches and propaganda emphasised the dictatorship of the proletariat.

407   On the other hand, quite a few parties whose programmes and speeches also said the dictatorship of the proletariat was their goal did, in fact, defend the cause of democracy in their concrete political struggles. They were, however, unable to establish the connection between these struggles and revolutionary struggles to transform society, and so remained in the bourgeoisie's shadow.

408   This situation has meant that the Marxist-Leninist Left has underrated democracy. When it has legitimately denounced the limits of representative or formal democracy, 'it has ended up by denying the importance of democracy itself',[205] forgetting that democratic gains are not a free gift from the bourgeoisie but the fruit of the historical struggles of popular movements, such as the struggle for universal suffrage, votes for women and the right to organise unions.

409   'A clear distinction hasn't always been made between formal and real democracy, between their mutual relationship, between what should be rejected and what should be saved.'[206]

An organisation which is the harbinger of the new society

410   An organisation which places its emphasis on the social practices of the different popular sectors rather than on the theory it contributes has to

be careful that its own practice does not contradict the values of the society it aims to create. In its inner workings, the organisation, as harbinger of the emancipated society, must take the lead in embodying the values of democracy, solidarity, cooperation, camaraderie. It must project vitality and joie de vivre.

411   In a world where corruption reigns and, as we saw earlier, political parties and politics in general have become increasingly discredited, it is essential that a Left organisation presents a distinctly different ethical profile; that, in its day-to-day existence, it is capable of practising the values it preaches; that its praxis is consistent with its political discourse, as Che's was. That explains why he is so attractive to young people, who are tired of a discourse that has nothing to do with the facts.

412   The people reject 'those churches which promise democracy for all social classes without discrimination but then deny their own congregation even the slightest freedom of expression when they don't blindly swallow their slogans ...; general staffs who, consulting no one, make pacts for everybody's welfare ...; giant organisational machines which steal the individual's initiative, words, and deeds ...'.[207]

413   And since the aim of the social revolution 'is not only to struggle for survival, but to transform one's way of life', as Nicaraguan sociologist Orlando Núñez says,[208] it is necessary for us to venture into the world of morality and of love searching for 'the direct, daily transformation of one's way of living, thinking and feeling',[209] by creating a new set of values. To wait for this to happen through a simple change in the relations of production is to bet on the mechanistic evolution we reject.

414   The new morality should tend to make the contradictions between social and individual values disappear by aspiring to build a world of cooperation, solidarity and love.

415   And this struggle to transform daily life should begin at the same time as a commitment to activism. There is no need to wait for the triumph of a social revolution since, as Che said, the 'individual subjects himself to a process of conscious self-education'.[210]

416   'The point is to learn how to struggle every day against all alienating institutions and structures, searching for a way to replace them [and] inventing new ones, which does not rule out struggling for big social and political transformations.'[211] If we struggle for the social liberation of women, we should begin as of now to transform the relationship between

man and woman in the heart of the family, to overcome the household division of labour and male-chauvinist culture at home. If we think that young people are the raw material of our work,[212] then we should educate them to think for themselves, to adopt their own positions and be capable of defending them, based upon what they feel and think. If we struggle against racial discrimination, we must carry that through into our own lives. If we struggle against the alienation caused by consumerism, then we should translate that into an austere lifestyle. One of the fundamental values that we must teach ourselves and others is that thought and action should be consistent with each other and double standards must be rejected. Che is one of the greatest examples of this.[213]

417   Moreover, it is essential that the organisation we build should embody the values of honesty and transparency. Any behaviour that tarnishes its image, even slightly, cannot be tolerated. The organisation should create a way to exercise strict vigilance over the honesty of its cadres and leaders.

418   Finally, I think a fourth value – moderation – must be added to the watchwords of the French Revolution- freedom, equality, and fraternity, which still apply today. This is not inspired by Christian asceticism, but by the need to oppose the suicidal and alienating consumerism of the late twentieth and early twenty-first centuries.

419   To sum up: in order to respond to the new challenges set by the twenty-first century we need a political organisation which, as it advances a national programme which enables broad sectors of society to rally round the same battle standard, also helps these sectors to transform themselves into the active subjects building the new society for which the battle is being waged.

Chapter 11
A New Paradigm for Internal Organisation

420   Thus far I have spoken about what are the most important characteristics essential to the organisation or political instrument we need to tackle the huge challenges set by the world today. Now we need to examine those things that have to do with this organisation's internal workings.

Unite your members around a community of values and a concrete programme

421   What unites the members of a political organisation should be mainly a 'cultural communion of values' from which they should derive their 'projects and programmes'.[214]

422   The political programme should be *the glue*, the unifying element par excellence, that which gives coherence to the organisation's political conduct. Whether we are talking about a Left political organisation or a more broadly based political front, the acceptance or not of the political programme should be the dividing line between those who are inside the organisation and those who choose to stay outside. There can be divergence over many things, but there must be consensus on questions concerning the programme.

423   There's a lot of talk about the unity of the Left. Without a doubt, unity is essential in order to move forward, but this is unity to struggle, unity to fight back, unity to transform. It is not just a unity of Left acronyms, since hidden among these acronyms there might be those who believe that we can do nothing else but adapt to the existing regime

and, if there are people like that, they will deplete the organisation's strength instead of adding to it.

424   It is important to realise that there are amounts that add to, amounts that take away from (like the example above) and *amounts that multiply*. The clearest example of the latter is Uruguay's Frente Amplio, a political coalition which brings together all the parties of the Uruguayan Left, and whose membership is markedly greater than the membership of all of the parties that comprise it. This unifying initiative by the Left successfully brought together a great number of people who previously did not belong to any of the parties that formed this coalition but who today participate in the Frente Amplio's Rank and File Committees. Two thirds of the Frente Amplio's members had no party affiliation; the remaining third were members of the constituent parties.

Contemplating different kinds of membership

Membership crisis and Left sensibility

425   Everybody knows that during the last few years there has been a generalised membership crisis, not only in Left political parties, but also in social movements and Christian Base Communities: it is not unrelated to the changes the world has undergone. However, in many of our countries this *membership crisis* has gone hand in hand with an increase in the Left's influence in society, and of *Left sensibility* in the popular sectors.

426   We think it very probable that the demands typically made on people before they can join in organised political activity are one factor that might have caused this crisis – that and the factors discussed above. We need to analyse whether or not the Left can create *different kinds of membership* in order to cultivate this increasing Left sensibility in society: not everybody has the same vocation for activism, or feels inclined to be active on a permanent basis. This fluctuates with the political times one lives in. Ignoring this fact and demanding a uniform kind of membership is self-limiting and weakens the political organisation.

Membership according to interest group, stable membership, and conjunctural membership

427   There are, for example, those who are willing to work in a specific area – such as health, education or culture – rather than in a cell in their

workplace or in a local organisation. There are others who feel called on to be active only at certain times (such as elections) but who are not prepared to be all year long, though at crucial junctures in the political struggle they can always be counted on and in their daily lives they promote the Left's project and values. Trying to fit membership into a single pigeonhole which is the same for everyone – a 24/7 kind of membership – leaves all these potential activists out in the cold.

428   We must create the kind of organisation which makes room for all the different types of membership, which allows varying degrees of commitment. Its structures must become more flexible in order to maximise this differentiated member commitment, without establishing a hierarchy of value among them. This will be, in some way, a network-type organisation.

429   Besides, I agree with Clodomiro Almeyda that the value and effectiveness of a person's political commitment should not be measured by their formal affiliation to a group, but by their *concrete contribution* to the promotion and development of the organisation's political projects and line.[215]

Adapting rank-and-file organisations to their environment

430   In order to make it easier to be a member in this differentiated way, structures and the rank-and-file organisations will have to be tailored to the kind of environment where they carry out their party work.[216] Clodomiro Almeyda considered that one valid criticism of Leninist party organisation was that it standardised the various levels of party structure without taking into account that every social environment is different. The cells or nuclei were structured in exactly the same way everywhere, without keeping in mind the specifics of each milieu: a factory isn't the same as a large rural estate or a university or a television channel.[217]

Collaborating with those who are not members

431   The political organisation should not confine itself to working with members who make a commitment to the party, but should also aim to work to include non-members in many tasks. One way to do so is by encouraging the creation or use of bodies that are not internal party structures. These can be useful to the political organisation, for example, by allowing it to take advantage of existing theoretical or technological skills such as research or advertising and publicity.

432   An interesting initiative along these lines is to bring together those persons – particularly experts – willing to contribute to the discussion of certain thematic questions such as agriculture, oil, housing, education and foreign debt. What used to be La Causa R (The R Cause) was involved in this kind of experiment in Venezuela during the last presidential electoral campaign. The FMLN in El Salvador has been trying this out since 1993, as has the EZLN in Mexico.

Activism as a way of life

433   The revolutionary struggle has tended to reduce the areas targeted for change to things related to the economy and the state, but little has been done to challenge the alienated culture and civilisation we live in; activists have forgotten that even under socialism 'the new society has to compete very fiercely against the past' because 'the failings of the past are handed down to the present in individual consciousness' and, therefore, 'a continuous effort has to be made to eradicate them'.[218]

434   'The principal battlefield of this struggle is daily life'.[219] For a long time, the political importance of everyday life has been undervalued. Daily life is not considered to be a political space in the broadest sense of the word.

435   'The transformation of daily life can only occur when the individual snatches or finds a space and time in his/her life in society for individuality.'[220] I think this proposal by Orlando Nuñez is very important, because if we cannot do what he suggests, then activists become dehumanised, lose their sensitivity and grow more and more distant from the rest of humanity. The struggle against individualism, a task that we should all devote ourselves to, does not mean denying the individual needs of each human being. 'Individual interests are not antagonistic to social ones; the one presupposes the other.'[221]

436   I also think it is necessary to change the mistaken relationship between activism and sacrifice. In the past to be an activist one had to have the mentality of a martyr: suffering was revolutionary, enjoying oneself was regarded as something suspicious.[222] In some way this was an echo of the collectivist deviation in real socialism: party members were just cogs in the party machinery; their individual interests were not taken into consideration. This does not mean that we don't appreciate revolutionary fervour, passion for activism, sense of duty, of rebellion, of responsibility

or the spirit of self-denial that activists must have, especially the leaders. Nevertheless, as far as is possible, they must strive to combine their duties as activists with developing the fullest possible personal life. And if the political tasks prevent them from having a more human life, they should be aware that this could result, as Che said, 'in extreme dogmatism, cold scholasticism and isolation from the masses'.[223]

437   I agree with Helio Gallardo that the classic Leftist practice – 'fundamentalist, serious, rigid, often heroic ... but also not very appealing to the people ... and frequently, sterile' – must be overcome.[224]

Giving up authoritarian methods

From bureaucratic centralism to democratic centralism

438   Left parties were very authoritarian for a very long time. What they practised was not democratic centralism, but Soviet-influenced bureaucratic centralisation.[225] The *general line of action* they followed was not previously discussed by all members and passed by a majority, but was decided on by the top leadership with no input from the members. The latter were limited to following orders that they had never discussed and often didn't understand.

439   But when combating this bureaucratic centralist deviation, efforts must be made to avoid slipping into *ultrademocratic* deviations which result in more talk than action, since everything, even trivial matters, are the subject of debate that frequently neuters any concrete action.

440   Because bureaucratic centralism has been criticised, there has been a tendency in recent years to reject all forms of centralism. This is reflected, for example, in the following quote from Immanuel Wallerstein: 'What the antisystemic forces should be concentrating on is the expansion of real social groups at community levels of every kind and variety and their grouping ... at higher levels in a nonunified form. The fundamental error of antisystemtic forces in the previous era was the belief that the more unified the structure, the more efficacious it was.... Democratic centralism is the exact opposite of what is needed. The basis of solidarity ... has to be subtler, more flexible, and more organic. The family of antisystemic forces must move at many speeds in constant reformulation of the tactical priorities.'

441   'Such a coherent, nonunified family of forces can only be plausible if

each constituent group is itself a complex, internally democratic structure. And this ... is possible only if, at the collective level, we recognize that there are no strategic priorities in the struggle.... The battle for transformation can only be fought on all fronts at once.'[226]

442   We agree with Wallerstein that the battle must be waged on many fronts. However, we do *not* agree that there is no need for the partial strategies of each sector to be coordinated into a general, single strategy at the most critical junctures in the struggle. It is this coordination which the enemy is most afraid of because they know that is where the strength of the anti-globalisation movement will lie.

443   Personally, I do not see how political action can be successful if it is not unified and for that reason I do not think that there is any method other than democratic centralism, unless a decision is taken to act by *consensus*. The consensus method appears to be more democratic because it tries to get everyone's agreement; but in practice it is sometimes much more anti-democratic, because it grants *veto power to a minority*, so that in extreme cases a single person can block the implementation of an agreement supported by the overwhelming majority. The best-known example of this is how the United States uses its veto in the UN Security Council. And anyway, the complexity of problems, the size of the organisation and the political timeframe – which means that at certain times decisions must be made quickly – often make it almost impossible to use the consensus method, even when it is not being used as blackmail.

There is no political effectiveness without unified leadership

444   There cannot be political effectiveness, then, without a unified leadership which defines the actions to be taken at various points in the struggle. This unified leadership is possible because it reflects a *general line of action* which has been discussed by all members of the organisation and approved by the majority. Those who are the minority must accept whatever course of action emerges triumphant and work with other members to carry out any tasks that it entails.

445   Nevertheless, if this general line is to be implemented, the concrete actions that the activists have to carry out must be identified. This must be done through a wide-ranging debate in which everyone is allowed to

give their opinion and where the agreements finally reached are binding on everyone. If there is to be a unified course of action, the lower levels of the organisation must keep the higher levels' instructions in mind when taking their own decisions. A political movement that seriously aspires to transform society cannot afford the luxury of harbouring undisciplined members who, in matters of strategic importance, disrupt its unity of action, without which no effective action is possible.

446   This combination of single central leadership and democratic debate at the organisation's various levels is called *democratic centralism*. It is a dialectical combination: in complicated political periods, periods of revolutionary upsurge or war, the balance tends to tip in the centralist direction; in periods of calm, when the rhythm of events is slower, the democratic character tends to come to the fore.

447   A correct combination of centrism and democracy should encourage the *initiative* of the leaders and all the members. Only creative action at every level of the party will assure the triumph of the class struggle. In practice, this initiative is manifested in a sense of responsibility, dedication to work, courage, and aptitude for problem solving, for expressing opinions, for criticising defects, and for exercising control – with comradely care – over higher-level bodies.

448   If this doesn't happen, the party as an organisation will cease to make sense because it fails to abide by the principle of internal democracy. An insufficiently democratic existence interferes with the creative initiative of the members and the consequence is their flagging participation.

Majorities and minorities

449   Democratic centralism implies both that the minority submit itself to the majority and that the majority respect the minority's position.

450   The minority must not be quashed or marginalised; it must be respected. Nor should the minority be required to completely submit to the majority.[227] The minority should submit itself to the *actions* proposed by the majority at concrete political junctures, but need not renounce its political, theoretical and ideological *convictions*. On the contrary, it is the minority's duty to continue fighting to defend its ideas until they convince the rest or are themselves convinced by others.

451   Why should the minority continue defending its positions and not capitulate to the majority position? Because the *minority might be right*:

their analysis of reality could be more accurate because they have been able to discover the true motivations of certain social actors. For this reason, those who are in the minority at a given time have not only the right but the duty to stick to their positions and fight to convert as many other members as possible to their positions through internal debate.

452   And anyway, if the majority is convinced that their position is correct then they have no reason to fear ideological struggle. On the contrary, they should welcome it, confident that they will succeed in convincing the minority group.

453   When the majority fears a confrontation it is because it feels weak because it senses that it is only a *formal majority*, and does not represent the *real majority* of the organisation's members.

454   Is this not the case of some Latin American revolutionary parties? Perhaps the truly *divisive* are not those who provoke the schism, but those who oblige the minority to take this way out if they want to do their duty of struggling against positions they believe to be wrong. How many schisms could have been avoided if the minority view had been respected? Instead, the whole weight of the bureaucratic apparatus was used to crush the minorities until they were left with no choice but to break away. And yet later those groups were accused of being divisive....

455   Thus far we've analysed the problem of minorities and majorities within political organisations. Now let's look at what can happen in a grassroots organisation. There can be a divergence or non-correspondence between representatives and represented and, as a result, even if a group is a minority, it might represent the interests of the real majority of people who belong to that organisation.

456   This divergence may come about for different reasons, such as the inherent incapacity of those who represent the real majority to achieve better representation in the grassroots organisation; the bureaucratic manoeuvres of the formal majority to keep itself in a position of power; rapid changes in the masses' consciousness because of the revolutionary process itself. For example, those who only a few days earlier did indeed represent the majority may have become only a formal majority because the revolutionary situation has caused the masses to see that the minority was right.

457   The correct way to resolve this contradiction will depend on the origin of this divergence.

458   To sum up, we can conclude that the problem of majorities and minorities goes beyond any quantitative analysis. Each one of these categories is relative. Often, majorities inside organisations are only formal majorities. What really matters is to remember *what these majorities and minorities represent with regard to the interests of the real majority*.

Creating spaces for debate

459   For the inner workings of an organisation to function democratically, it is vital that it create spaces where members can debate, consolidate positions, and become enriched through exchanging opinions.

460   To date, except for rare exceptions, party cells or nuclei have been the preferred space in the organisation for exercising internal party democracy. However, it is obvious this is a very limited space in which to examine certain questions in depth, especially those concerned with establishing the general party line and the lines for different sectors. Larger meetings seem much richer – meetings where good speakers can come together to get to the root of their differences, which in turn helps the others present to form their own political beliefs. It is a way to begin to encourage people to *think for themselves*.

461   How could anyone think, for example, that a debate about the country's economic situation and the line to take on this could be discussed in workplace or local cells or nuclei? Doesn't new thinking emerge through debate? What kind of debate can you have in a group of ten, twenty or thirty people who don't have a thorough understanding of the subject? Wouldn't it make more sense to get the party's main experts together and have them debate the issue so the other members can hear them state their positions – and then make up their own minds?

462   Finding the most appropriate mechanisms for improving democratic debate inside political organisations is one of the challenges facing the Left.

Currents of opinion, yes, factions, no

463   It is entirely normal that different opinions exist within a political organisation; these are in fact only a reflection of the different political sensibilities of its members.[228] Besides, I think that the organisation's thinking can be enriched if members form groups around given positions. What must be avoided is that these currents of opinion become closed

groups or factions: in other words, veritable parties within the party.[229] Something else to avoid is letting the theoretical debates become the excuse for a power struggle over something that has nothing to do with the question being debated. The former can be achieved through internal legislation that recognises the right to have different opinions but which imposes sanctions on factions.

464   On the other hand, if the goal is to democratise debate, then the most logical thing would be not to have permanent groups, and, at least on some questions (especially new questions), to allow people to move between groups. For example, the people who take a given position on the role of the state in the economy will not always be in the same group as those who take a particular position on how the party should encourage women to get politically involved.

465   And while we are on the subject, I think that in the 1990s there was an excellent example of democratic praxis in Porto Alegre, Brazil. In the city government the mayor's job is rotated through the various ideological tendencies of the PT and each mayor forms his or her staff by selecting representatives of the various tendencies.

466   The new praxis is only possible if one assumes that the positions taken by the current one belongs to 'will have to be complemented by the dialectic of dialogue and debate with others. Otherwise, if one takes the old traditional position that one represents the proletariat and everyone else is an enemy', then one's attitude will automatically be different: these others will have to be either 'neutralized or crushed'.[230]

467   This is only possible if one starts out by acknowledging that one does not possess the whole truth, that others might possess some of the truth and that their positions, therefore, are legitimate. If the dialogue and the debate fail to lead to an understanding, consensus, then differences must be resolved through a vote. But this would only work if all involved are willing to submit themselves to the results of the vote. Tarso Genro says that 'this is the bedrock on which to build the political culture of a modern socialist party, a revolutionary, non-autocratic party that doesn't propose to bureaucratically impose its program upon society or even on itself'.[231]

468   Now, being open, respectful and flexible in debate does not in any way mean refusing to fight for one's own ideas if one is in the minority. If members remain convinced after the process of internal debate that

their ideas are correct, then they should continue defending those ideas, as long as they also respect the need to preserve the party's unity when acting upon decisions reached by the majority.

469   And, speaking of debate, it is important to recognise that today it is almost impossible to have an internal debate that is not also a public debate, so the Left must learn how to debate keeping this in mind.

Building leadership that respects the internal composition of the party

470 The new Left culture should also be reflected in a different way of constituting the political organisation's leadership. For a long time it was believed that if a certain tendency or sector of the party won the internal elections by a majority, then their cadres should occupy all the leadership positions. To a certain extent this was because the generally accepted idea was that a party can only govern when the leadership is as homogeneous as possible. Today different opinions tend to predominate; it is thought that leaders who accurately reflect the *internal correlation of forces* within the party are better because this helps members from all tendencies to feel more involved in party work. But this opinion can only become effective if the party has managed to acquire the new democratic culture: if it hasn't, then bedlam will result and render the party ungovernable.

471   Real democratisation of the political organisation demands that members participate more effectively in electing their leaders, who should be elected according to their ideological and political positions rather than their personal attainments. It is important, therefore, that these different positions are made known to party members through internal publications. It is also very important to find a more democratic way of deciding on candidates and of ensuring elections are held in a way that guarantees the secret vote.

Internal plebiscites and polls

472 On the other hand, I think the direct participation of the party members in the most important decisions is a good idea and can be implemented through a process of *internal plebiscites* or polls.[232] And I stress 'the most important decisions', since there is no sense in consulting the membership about decisions regarding day-to-day, routine business which does not necessarily need rank-and-file input – and, anyway, it would be

unworkable. Direct polling of the party's support base, however, is a very effective way to democratise the organisation's decision-making process.

The political organisation polls the people

473   Polls of the sort just mentioned can be taken, not only of party members, but also of party sympathisers or of those whom we could call its potential electoral support. This method is especially useful for nominating left-wing candidates for local government, if the point is to actually win the election and not just use it as an opportunity to promote the party's ideas. Polling the electorate about the various candidates proposed by the political organisation is the best way to avoid missing the mark. Elections have been lost in the past because candidates were chosen for purely internal party reasons – prestige in the party, representation of a given internal correlation of forces – without taking the public's opinion about the candidate into account.

474   The people have been successfully consulted in Latin America. For example, La Causa R (The R Cause) in Venezuela held a popular referendum a few months after the military coup led by Lieutenant Colonel Hugo Chávez and his Bolivarian Movement. In this poll – taken by placing ballot boxes on the main streets of Caracas – people were asked if they thought the then-president of the republic, Carlos Andrés Pérez, should continue to govern or not. Of the 500,000 people who voted, most of them from the metropolitan region, 90 per cent were against his continuing as president. This referendum helped to create a political situation in favour of the president's resignation, leading to a new political reality in the country: this was the first time that parliament had asked a president to leave office and be judged before his term was up. No law provided for this type of consultation, but neither did any law prohibit it. The mass participation of the people – although the results were not formally recognised – was in itself a political event.

475   Another example is provided by the consultations carried out by the EZLN in Mexico. Approximately 1.3 million people participated in the National Consultation for Peace and Democracy carried out by the Zapatista Civilian Movement in the second half of 1995. This highly original consultation focused on various topics of interest, which included whether or not the Zapatista organisation should unite with others and form a political front or remain an independent organisation. The most

recent consultation – The International Consultation for the Recognition of the Rights of the Indian Peoples and for an End to the War of Extermination – held on 21 March 1999, saw citizen participation double to close to three million voters.

476   Examples such as these make me think that the Left has a tendency to move through the dichotomy between the legal and the illegal, but often fails to pay attention to countless other spaces that I would denominate *a-legal*, since they don't fit into the above dichotomy. These spaces can be used in a very creative way to raise consciousness, mobilise people and have them participate in a way that builds the anti-system social force that we've mentioned before.

Giving pluralism its due

477   The political organisation that we've been speaking about should be democratic not only internally, but externally as well. It should recognise the importance of supra-party initiatives 'without underestimating the decisive importance of renovating and empowering party organisations.'[233]

A political organisation for those exploited and excluded by capitalism

478   If, as we mentioned above, the numbers of the traditional industrial working class in Latin America have been declining – as opposed to those of workers who have unstable, insecure jobs and to the marginalised or excluded by the system, whose numbers go up every day – the political body must recognise this fact and cease to be an organisation solely for the traditional working class; it must transform itself into an organisation for all the oppressed.

A political organisation which is not naïve but is preparing itself for any eventuality

479   The opportunity that the Left now has to compete openly and legally for spaces must not lead it to forget that the Right only respects the rules of the game as long as it suits its purposes to do so. To date, there has never been a single example anywhere in the world of a ruling group that has given up its privileges willingly. The fact that its members agree to

withdraw from the political arena when they think their retreat may be in their best interests shouldn't deceive us. They may tolerate and even help bring a Left government to power if that government implements the Right's policies and limits itself to managing the crisis. What the Right will always try to prevent – and we should have no illusions about this – is any attempt to build an alternative society.[234]

480   It may be deduced from this that as the Left grows and begins to occupy positions of power, it must be prepared to confront fierce resistance from the sectors closest to finance capital who will use legal or illegal means to block a democratic transformation that will benefit the people. The Left must be capable of defending victories achieved democratically.

481   It is essential to remember, as the British Marxist theorist Perry Anderson[235] says in reference to bourgeois democracies, that 'in the most tranquil democracies today, the army may remain invisible in its barracks [but] the "fundamental" resort of bourgeois class power, beneath the "preponderant" cusp of culture in a parliamentary system, remains coercion'. History has shown this to be essential, and therefore, when a revolutionary crisis develops in the heart of the bourgeois power structure, the dominant class of necessity moves from 'ideology to violence. Coercion becomes both determinant and dominant in the supreme crisis, and the army inevitably occupies the front of the stage in any class struggle against the prospect of a real inauguration of socialism.'[236]

482   Being aware of this situation does not necessitate a return to the clandestine methods of the time of the dictatorships; these are no longer valid given the processes of democratic liberalisation that Latin America is experiencing today. Yet it seems necessary not to abandon methods of self-defence when circumstances warrant it, and to do good intelligence work so as to find out what the enemy is planning and to prepare a response ahead of time.

483   If the forces of the Right had respected the people's legally achieved victories, and if the Left had had the same opportunities as the Right to reach the masses through the mass media, I have no doubt that the Left would have preferred to travel down the road of institutional struggle. But, historically it is the Right, and not the Left, that has closed off this road.

484   On the other hand, Gramsci taught us that *military effects are not only achieved through armed actions*, which, because of the 'democratic' system

that exists in some countries, are difficult for the majority of the population to understand. He distinguished between the strictly military or the *techno-military* and the *politico-military*. It is necessary to keep in mind that *certain political actions can have military effects on the enemy*. These include, for example, causing troops to be spread out across the country or weakening their fighting morale. Gramsci called these actions 'politico-military' because, in spite of being entirely political, they could potentially produce military effects.[237]

New internationalist practice for the globalised world

485   In a world in which domination is exercised on a global level, it seems even more necessary than before to coordinate strategies of resistance on a regional and supra-regional level. The world social fora and other international meetings have made significant advances in this direction possible – but there is still a lot left to do.

486   What Enrique Rubio pointed out in 1994 is still totally relevant today: we should try to coordinate all 'the excluded, overlooked, dominated, and exploited in the world', including those who live in developed countries; a kind of coordination, cooperation, and alliance between 'all political and social subjects who take part in the struggle for emancipation' in an effort to build world identities. We need to elaborate 'a strategy that includes coordinating with forces that operate in the three great world power blocs', and to establish multilateral relations with each one of them as a way to 'disrupt the political sharing of zones of influence among them'.

487   'It is essential to put capitalism in check from the political sphere, whether the state or non-state, activist or non-activist, party or non-party, from social movements, from scientific-technical centres, through cultural and communication centres, where sensibilities are constructed in a decisive manner, and put it in check from self-management organisations … or to put it in a slightly schematic and perhaps even shocking way, the revolution must be international, democratic, multiple and profound, or there won't be a revolution.'[238]

PART IV
From Reforms to Revolution:
The Bolivarian Revolutionary Process

Chapter 12
Local Governments: Signposts to an Alternative Path

488   I have spoken above of the crucial role that local governments can play in Left strategy. But not everyone on the Left shares my view of the tremendous importance of the work done in local governments. The more radical sectors are very sceptical about the role these governments can play in accumulating forces for social change. They claim that what these governments do is simply 'manage' capitalism; that they only serve as shock absorbers for neo-liberal policies; and what is more, they accuse them of attempting to co-opt the leaders of the popular movement, so that instead of the movement being strengthened by the experience it is in fact weakened.

489   These sectors believe that the conditions for an insurrection could arise and that what we have to do is demolish the bourgeois state; in other words, they believe that the revolution is at hand. Those of us, on the other hand, who believe that we are living in an ultra-conservative era and are at a great disadvantage with regard to the local and global balance of power also believe that what it boils down to is that we have to begin to act within existing structures with the aim of changing them; we therefore view running a local government as something positive. We look on it, moreover, as a space that could also be used to create the cultural and political conditions needed if we are to advance towards an autonomous organisation of society.

490   Next I would like to spend some time looking at the social experiments that a sector of the Latin American Left has been carrying out in various municipal governments there.

491   I am referring to eight experiences of municipal administration: the Montevideo City Council under Uruguay's Frente Amplio;[239] five municipalities governed by the Brazilian Workers Party,[240] and two by the former La Causa R of Venezuela.[241] I chose these particular cases because they were not 'sniper' governments – rather, they represented political party or political front projects that gave them their own 'look' and allowed an outside observer to identify them as expressions of a particular political organisation.[242]

492   Here I shall make a first attempt, which will have to be expanded on later, to systematise these experiences.

493   These opinions stem in large part from the perception that exists about the current political situation and the role attributed to the state in that situation.

494   But in order that Left governments embody a truly alternative practice, it is necessary to differentiate them sharply from authoritarian regimes of the Right and from populist governments, of the Right or Left, that have been and continue to be the most common in Latin America.

495   I have been able to study some local governments in Latin America which have set out to arrange things so that the people can play *a protagonistic role* and thus overcome the traditional and profoundly undemocratic style of government that concentrates power in the hands of the few and ignores the overwhelming majority of the population while making decisions for it.

496   What it entails is implementing a way of exercising power at the local level which will fight against traditional problems such as abuses of power, clientism and clinging to political power for long periods of time – a way of governing which, above all, *delegates power to the people* which is why I have called these city governments *popular participation governments*.

497   They are also guided by Artigas's motto: *the downtrodden must be the privileged ones*. Their priority is to find solutions for those who were always humiliated and needy without abandoning their concern for the city as a whole. They try to reverse the priorities in order to pay the accumulated social debt to the most destitute sectors without abandoning those who were always well served. Their administrative practice is completely transparent and they give an account of their activities to the citizens at regular intervals.

498   These are also governments that believe the state can play a valuable

role in providing services to the population. They believe that the state's role need not be reduced; rather, it needs to be de-privatised. In other words, they want to prevent the state apparatus from being used in the interests of a privileged few. What they do, therefore, is to democratise it.

499 It is interesting to note that governments that have been formed by such diverse political associations – the Brazilian Workers' Party is a mass party with deep roots among industrial workers and peasants; the Frente Amplio of Uruguay is a political front made up of different Left parties and independents; and the former La Causa R of Venezuela was a party/movement of cadres[243] – have all experienced similar problems and have found very similar ways to solve them without having previously shared experiences. Let us now examine some of these initiatives.

The problem of knowing how to govern

500 One of the first problems that these governments face when they assume power is that of knowing how to govern, a problem that was completely unknown to a Left used to being the eternal opposition. They have often won elections with the idea of forming a government composed exclusively of workers, but they soon realise that such a move would make things unworkable. Apart from isolating them socially and politically, such a move would have a direct repercussion in parliament, where legislation on the basic reforms – taxes, the budget, etcetera – that allow them to govern is passed.

501 In many cases, the right to govern is won by a relative majority – a mayor can be elected with little more than a third of the votes. It is also unlikely that there will be a favourable balance of power in the legislative chamber during the first term in office. This means that, initially, a majority of the people do not share the Left's political project and a way to govern under those conditions has to be found. The only way to do this is by building alliances,[244] which the more radical sectors of the Left have difficulty understanding.

502 This policy of forming alliances revolves around a political proposal for governing the city, one that embodies the interests of the majority and opposes these to the interests of a privileged minority. This minority usually opposes the plan and attempts to sabotage it; but there have been

social sectors with which the Left was able to negotiate as well as others that it was only able to neutralise. The natural base of support for these governments is the popular sectors but they haven't always supported them at the beginning. It is important to remember that in Latin America and the Caribbean, the Right manages to get a lot of votes from the most oppressed sectors. However, there tends to be a significant increase in support for the Left by these sectors when they see that the new governments really are on the people's side, in deed and not just in word.

503 Experience has taught local governments that the degree of hegemony achieved is not measured by the number of people that the political organisation has in the administration, but by the number of people who feel that this organisation's political project understands their needs. And this translates, at the governmental level, into a non-sectarian attitude that gives positions in the government to those who are best qualified for the job, even if they are independents or people from other parties in the coalition that helped to win the election.

504 Anyway, the city governments studied used three methods in order to obtain enough votes to get their projects through the municipal legislature, where the representatives of the Leftist coalition were in a minority. The *first* consisted of proposing well-thought-out, attractive draft legislation that was enthusiastically received by the public – and thus could not be rejected by opposition council members if they wanted to keep their electoral support. The second consisted of direct negotiation with the council members from different parties to get them to include the municipal government's proposals in their own projects. The third consisted in mobilising social sectors that were interested in particular projects so that they themselves pressured the council.

505 Of course, it would be best to have a majority on the town council. Election campaigns now stress that it is not enough to elect just the mayor; a majority in the municipal legislature must be elected too. The problem of alliances moves then to the election arena: a broader electoral alliance ensures a better balance of power in the council.

The party's weakness vis-à-vis the government

506 One of the problems common to all of these political experiences is that when the Left wins a local government for the first time, the grassroots

and political organisations' best cadres are immediately drained away into the government. These cadres are called upon to accept management or advisory jobs in the various government departments. Through the new institutional tasks and enormous difficulties they face if they are to implement a programme for an alternative government, they gain experience in a previously unknown area: they learn how the state apparatus works, how it is organised. They realise that winning the government is not the same as winning power; at first hand and for the first time they see how the much-criticised bureaucratic apparatus that they have inherited places tremendous obstacles in the way of a transformative project. This makes them mature. They quickly learn that it is *one thing to be the opposition and quite another to be the government*.

507   For their part, the political organisations – debilitated by the loss of their cadres, powerless to follow the rhythm of decision making required by an executive body of this kind and unable to understand the difference between being the opposition and being the government – instead of playing the role of guide to the new government's actions, tend to adopt an attitude of critical opposition, at times even harsher than that of the Right. This explains why the relationships between these governments and their respective political groupings have not always been the most harmonious, at least not during the initial period.[245]

508   Experience has led us to conclude that they require a *party mediating body at the highest level* – national or state – to resolve the differences that often arise between municipal political leaders; and a *political team that looks beyond day-to-day affairs*, that considers the big picture and that, at given intervals, critically evaluates the way the government is going so it can correct its course in time if it has lost its way, or if new situations arise that demand an unplanned change of direction.

509   Although the government should have autonomy from the party, this cannot be complete autonomy; it cannot extend to questions of principle since what the government does reflects on the party. There doesn't have to be consultation over every decision – things need to be workable and the rhythm of a town council is much more dynamic than that of a party – but the general line to be followed should be discussed collectively.

510   Since that margin of autonomy allows the government to implement measures with which the political organisation does not agree but for which, in the public's eyes, it is equally responsible, it faces the dilemma

of either being openly critical in order to make it clear who *is* responsible – knowing that this will be used by the Right to discredit the government – or appearing committed to a policy that is not party policy.

511　　The political organisation must be sufficiently mature to make public criticisms that are not merely destructive. It is important that they indicate how mistakes can be corrected. If this does not happen, public criticism ends up being counterproductive and ultimately weakens popular government.

The bureaucratic apparatus and how to contend with it

The legacy

512　One of the biggest challenges facing these inexperienced governments is how to bring the bureaucratic apparatus that they inherit under control.[246] In addition to the legal obstacles, the economic difficulties, and the hostility of central governments which have absolutely no interest in supporting them, there is the problem of too many government employees, the result of political clientism; the unwillingness of senior civil servants[247] to change their habits because they are used to the old style of working; and the lack of will of those who do not agree politically with the administration. It becomes increasingly evident that 'it is not enough to change the driver yet still drive the same vehicle along the bumpy road of popular participation. The vehicle must be changed too.'[248]

513　　And then, these governments must fight the neo-liberal thesis that the state is *per se* inefficient and must therefore be downsized by privatising public services. Left governments must, therefore, show themselves to be efficient, and to that end must rationalise and modernise services without laying off government employees.

Rationalisation and modernisation without lay-offs

514　This is, undoubtedly, a complex problem that cannot be solved with good intentions alone. Nevertheless, some of these municipal governments have undertaken interesting experiments. They have been able to modernise without creating unemployment by recycling workers who are retrained and relocated to other jobs. By doing this, municipal governments prove that a humanist concern with defending workers' living conditions does not mean there is no possibility of modernising state enterprises and public services.

Correcting the poor geographical distribution of public services

515 In some municipalities, the problem has not been too many employees in certain departments or services, but their poor geographical distribution. Often, particularly in big cities, sectors of the population are deprived of municipal services because they live a long way from the centre of the city – many public officials are not willing to provide services in outlying districts. One way this problem was resolved was to hold a public competitive examination for people who did not belong to the municipal system, and to decide on where they would be located geographically according to marks obtained in the exam. Those who obtained the highest marks could choose where they wanted to work, the rest had to go where they were sent or lose their chance of a job. Parallel to this measure, the municipality decided to give an incentive to those who chose to work in the outlying locations by paying a 'distance allowance' which varied according to how far away the workplace was from the centre.[249]

Wage demands and scarce resources

516 How to manage personnel has been one of the most difficult things to learn.

517 Typically, Left political organisations have learned management skills in the context of union demands, often with a somewhat economistic orientation. Traditionally, the best leaders have been those who have achieved the greatest material gains for the workers. On top of this, the poor conditions in which *municipal* workers generally found themselves created high expectations when the Left gained control of local governments. The result is increasing pressure from local government employees for a wage increase. Left-controlled local governments are very sensitive to this situation: they know that a fair wage is a way for those workers to recover their dignity. How can these governments resolve this situation with the limited material resources at hand and at the same time allocate resources for social projects to meet the needs of the destitute?

518 There have been two interesting initiatives in this area. The first involves *linking wage increases to revenue increases*, with the aim of creating awareness among municipal workers that their work is part of a much

bigger whole – the city and its needs. At the same time, when pointing out this connection, the aim is to make them into staunch allies for raising taxes and generally improving the municipality's revenues. As services improve, people will be more willing to pay taxes.

519   Another interesting initiative has been the formation of *tripartite commissions* of management, public employees and popular movements to hold collective discussions on wage policy for public employees. Popular movements are very well aware of the need for public employees to earn better wages, but this understanding does not mean that they are willing to renounce the public works projects they need. In return for agreeing to this, the movements demand that public employees provide better services. Public servants must understand that the best defence of public services is their quality, because it is the public who, if well served, will join municipal employees in defending those services from privatisation.

Involving public servants in the decision-making process

520   Moreover, these administrations have realised that the shortcomings of and lack of discipline among civil servants will not be overcome through top-down authoritarianism and the implementation of repressive controls. What has been done is to discuss the measures to be taken with the civil servants themselves because *if people are involved in taking decisions, they feel engaged and committed*. The attitude that the administration has toward the workers is of vital importance in making them feel equally responsible for the services they provide and willing to work with greater efficiency. The major challenge these mayors faced was how to gain respect without being authoritarian and how to combine this with respect for the autonomy that social movements should have. They had to learn how to find the right solution to the contradiction between having to facilitate workers' self-organisation and mobilisation – even when the aim of that mobilisa- tion might be to criticise the town council and put pressure on it to concede workers' demands – and, at the same time, to maintain their own authority in the eyes of the public, since it is impossible to govern without authority and respect. This challenge is huge, because if union leaders are from the Right, they often try to cause problems for a Left government.

521   When concern is shown for public employees' working conditions and living standards, when their contribution to society is appreciated and when they are able to recover their dignity, their self-image changes, their

self-esteem improves and this in turn has a positive effect on their efficiency. Similarly, as civil servants improve the quality of their service they get more job satisfaction and the public's opinion of them improves. This shows in many ways and is a great incentive for continuing to improve the service.

Popular participation in the government

Initial difficulties

522   As has already been stated, the municipal governments referred to here have set themselves the goal of creating a social project in which civil society, and particularly the popular sectors, are the protagonists. So, to live up to their avowed aims once in power, they have had to find formulas that allow people to participate in the administration – by, for instance, discussing what measures to adopt, setting priorities, and keeping an eye on what the government and its departments do. Along with creating institutional spaces for popular participation, they have also had to encourage the people's autonomous organisation – the only guarantee that the strategic project of a socialist society will be viable in the future.

523   This has not been an easy task.[250] When these popular governments triumphed, they were greeted not only by a great deal of apathy and scepticism among the people but also by popular movements that were weak, fragmented and depoliticised. They also found a people not used to thinking politically but accustomed to populism, political clientism and asking for things. In the popular assemblies that were organised a list of requests would often be drawn up and these usually greatly exceeded the municipality's ability to satisfy them.

524   That experience led these governments to conclude that *not all assemblies are synonymous with democracy*; that assemblies are not productive if people don't have adequate information, or are not politicised. So politicisation became the main problem. To expand democracy, it was necessary to politicise.[251] 'The problem was how to reach the people', said the former mayor of Caracas, Aristóbulo Istúriz, 'how to help the most disadvantaged citizens to become politicised and acquire the ability to make decisions. To do so, it was essential to provide the people with information: democracy can only exist when all people are equally informed.'[252]

Things to keep in mind

525   A serious problem these governments face is reaching people, not just activists. When they attempt to get in contact with the people, they only meet activists: the worker who is the president of a neighbourhood association, or the housewife who is a leader in her community. Often they are activists who are politicised, yes, but badly politicised, since they are still burdened by the worst vices and shortcomings of the traditional political system: populism, caciquism, verticalism, corruption, and manipulation of popular movements. What, then is to be done to really reach the people and get them involved in state administration?

526   One of the things these governments learned is that *it is vital to begin with the immediate needs of the people* and, though it might seem like a truism, it must be emphasised that we are talking about the *people's* needs – not what we think their needs are.

527   It is also important that those heading the government and all those who are trying to get the communities organised know *how to listen and how to be flexible enough to accept people's opinions – even if they are different from their own*. There might be valid technical criteria about where, for example, to locate a bus stop, but the population might think otherwise. If the experts are unable to convince people with their arguments, the people will feel that their sovereignty has been trampled on. Besides, expert opinions are not always right.

528   If people are to participate, there must be a *minimum level of community organisation and a minimum amount of technical and material resources* with which to implement the ideas that emerge. This is why the self-management experiences of some of the municipalities are important.

529   Finally, it is essential to have *complete confidence in the people's creative initiative*, since they might find solutions that have not occurred to the administration.

The participatory budget: the key to participation and politicisation

530   In all the administrations that I have studied, the master key to reaching people at the grassroots level, to motivating them to participate in municipal government, has been convening them to discuss and decide

which public projects in the municipality – depending on its resources – should be given priority. The Brazilian Workers Party (PT) has given the name 'the participatory budget' to this process, where the people participate in deciding how to allocate municipal resources. PT local governments have the most experience with the participatory budget.[253]

531   The novelty of the participatory budget lies in the fact that it is not simply the experts and those who govern who decide, behind closed doors, about revenues and public spending. It is the community which, through a process of debates and consultations, sets the amounts of revenues and expenditures and decides where to invest, what the priorities should be and which actions and public works the government will undertake. That is why the budget is participatory.[254]

532   It is interesting to observe that the traditional logic of public resource allocation – that had always benefited the wealthier sectors – is transformed through this process of discussing the allocation of local government resources to public works with residents. By encouraging popular participation, especially that of the neediest sectors, the participatory budget emerges as a powerful tool for distributing the city's revenue more equitably.

533   The participatory budget also becomes an instrument for planning and for controlling the administration.

534   The problem of control is perhaps one of the most overlooked, but, at the same time, one of the most essential issues if things are to be done in a democratic way. It is pointless to decide on priorities and allocate resources to given works if people are not organised to follow up on those initiatives: to make sure that the resources are used for their designated purposes and not diverted to other things; and that the quality of public works carried out is high.

535   The lack of organised control by the community is what leads not only to corruption and the misuse of funds, but also to members of the community not doing what they need to do to further the collective interest.

536   The Caroní municipal government talked of giving democratic back-up to public works. The people who use a sports field do not only participate in repairing or building it; they also organise to maintain and look after it, and to ensure that the rules they themselves have established to prevent its deterioration are respected.

537   The participatory budget is also a very effective tool in the struggle

against clientism and favour swapping. Since the community itself chooses the public projects, the influence of top bureaucrats, council members and local bosses over the distribution of resources is neutralised.

538   It is, moreover, an effective way of oiling the wheels of the machinery of administration, making it more competent and reducing the bureaucracy. It also increases the level of satisfaction when the public works are completed, minimising the demand for more works while simultaneously improving the quality of life. And then, when people see efficiency and transparency in the way their taxes are used, they are more willing to pay them and less likely to engage in tax evasion. Finally, perhaps the most significant achievement is that citizens have been successfully motivated to participate in the tasks of municipal government. The fact that the residents in a community learn about and decide on public issues is a concrete way for people to govern. It makes them grow as human beings: it dignifies them – people no longer feel like beggars – and it politicises them in the broadest sense of that word, allowing them to have their own opinions which can no longer be manipulated. Increasingly, it makes them the subject of their own destiny.

539   According to Tarso Genro, this process makes it possible to break with the traditional alienation of the community leaders, who think that their problem is one that affects their street and neighbourhood only. People begin to understand that their problems are related to the overall situation of the economy, the national social situation, and even to the international situation. This has nothing to do with the state co-opting popular organisations or dissolving them into itself. On the contrary, a concentration of power outside the state, outside the executive, and outside the legislature is created. That is why I believe the participatory budget is a *highly positive and highly revolutionary experience*.

540   It is reinforced, moreover, by the many other initiatives these municipal governments undertake, which are creating more and more spaces for popular participation. Nowadays, in Porto Alegre for example, there are dozens of fora apart from the Participatory Budget Council, the most famous because it mobilises the most oppressed and exploited sectors of society. It shares the new participatory space with the Citizenship Council, the Councils against Discrimination and Racism, the Municipal Culture Council, the Municipal Health Council, the Social Assistance

Council and the Tutelary Councils. Direct citizen participation is exercised through all of these.

541   In conclusion, I would like to state my conviction that, at a time when politics and politicians have been widely discredited, something which also affects Left parties, local governments run by a transformative Left can be a very potent weapon because they offer an example of something other than neo-liberalism; they demonstrate to people that the Left 'not only claims to be better but actually is better'.[255] No less important: they can give us, as I said at the beginning of this chapter, a preview of an alternative route.

542   Their responsibility, therefore, is huge; what is at stake is not only the people's dreams, but also the political future of the Left.

Chapter 13
The Left and Reform

Has the Left become reformist?

543 Does the fact that growing sectors of the Latin American Left have concentrated their efforts on institutional spaces in the last few years mean that a majority of this Left has become reformist?

544   In order to answer this question we must first answer some other questions: is a Left which concentrates on things institutional necessarily reformist? Is a Left which rejects things institutional and proposes very radical solutions necessarily revolutionary? Are those who today are in favour of advancing via reforms reformist?

545   In order to begin, it seems to me important to reflect upon something someone wrote decades ago: 'The greatest, perhaps the only danger to the genuine revolutionary is that of exaggerated revolutionism, of *ignoring the limits* and conditions in which revolutionary methods are appropriate and can be successfully employed.' These are not the words of a social democrat; they are the words of a revolutionary – none other than Lenin himself. He went on to develop his idea in these words: 'True revolutionaries have mostly come a cropper when they began to write 'revolution' with a capital R, to elevate 'revolution' to something almost divine, to lose their heads, to lose the ability to reflect, weigh and ascertain in the coolest and most dispassionate manner *at what moment, under what circumstances and in which sphere of action* you must act in a revolutionary manner, and *at what moment, under what circumstances and in which sphere you must turn to reformist action*'.[256]

Distinction between revolution and reform

546   The distinction between reformists and revolutionaries is not always clear, because – as Norberto Bobbio says – 'reform is not always advocated in order to avoid revolution, nor is revolution necessarily linked to the use of violence'.[257] When these positions are developed to their logical conclusion, it is easier to distinguish between them, but in day-to-day political practice it is much harder to do so.

547   In fact, the founders of Marxism were always in favour of the battle for reforms, although they knew that 'reform is the name given to changes which leave the power in the country in the hands of the old ruling class'.[258]

548   The problem is not saying yes or no to reform, but examining *when* it makes sense to fight for reform and *how* revolutionary fruit can be plucked from it.[259]

549   In conclusion, neither the use of violence, on the one hand, nor the use of institutions and the promotion of reform, on the other, can be used as the criteria for drawing a line of demarcation between revolution and reform.

550   What criteria should be used, then?

551   It seems to me that the best definition is one which pins the label *reformist* on those who wish to improve the existing order through reform, and that of *revolutionary* on those who, although pushing for reform, fight at the same time to modify that order profoundly, to bring about a change that cannot happen without a break with the previously existing order.

Conditions needed if the institutional struggle is to achieve revolutionary ends

552   How is it possible to detect if a political practice that uses reform and takes the institutional route is reformist or revolutionary, especially when self-proclaimed objectives mean less and less in politics?

553   I propose the following criteria to determine just how revolutionary a political practice is:

554   *First:* if the reforms advocated are accompanied by a *parallel effort to strengthen the popular movement*, in such a way that growing sectors of the people organise and join the struggle.

555   *Second: if lessons can be learned and taught* when the Left works within the

existing institutional framework. An electoral campaign, for example, can be an excellent space for popular education, provided that the campaign is expressly geared to increasing the people's awareness of the most important political questions. However, a campaign can also be reduced to a simple exercise in marketing which, instead of raising consciousness, disorients the people or simply does not add anything to their political maturity.

556   *Third:* if the political practice is *different*, one that makes it impossible to confuse the Left's behaviour and that of traditional political parties. It should also reflect an effort to *expose the limits* of existing institutions and the *need to change them*, but without raising hopes about the path of reform being able to solve problems that demand revolutionary solutions.

557   I agree with Carlos Vilas that 'the challenge faced by organisations which in the past resorted to armed struggle or intense political confrontations is related to their ability and willingness to remain true to the proposals for profound change in the new institutional scenario. A scenario which demands that adjustments be made in style, rhythm and strategy, but should not, in principal, involve changes in substantive concepts or in the scope of alternative proposals.'[260]

Varieties of reformism

558   On the other hand, the following could be used as indications of reformist deviations:

559   *First:* a *tendency to moderate programmes and initiatives* without offering 'alternative political proposals to the existing order',[261] justifying this with the argument – analysed above – that politics is the art of the possible.

560   *Second:* instead of investing time and effort in fomenting rebellion and a fighting spirit, constantly calling on 'leaders of unions and the workers' movement to conduct themselves' responsibly and with maturity.[262] This includes trying to channel their efforts towards negotiations and shady deals at the top and to avoid combative demonstrations under the pretext of not wanting to put a spanner in the works of the state apparatus or to jeopardise the hard-won rebirth of democracy.

561   The opportunistic slogan *don't make waves* clearly expresses this situation. And, as Carlos Vilas says: 'far from encouraging a creative search for alternatives, this slogan instead works to block all projects for change

and adapt their content and scope to spaces tolerated by the institutional system....'[263]

562   *Third:* the *tendency to work in existing institutions passively*, without fighting to change them or to change the rules of the game.

563   How many times have we heard the Left complain about the adverse conditions in which it had to fight the elections after discovering that it had not achieved the results it expected at the polls? However, this same Left has very rarely denounced the rules of the game during the election campaign or included electoral reform in their platform. Quite the reverse; what often happens is that in its hunt for votes the Left, instead of waging an educational, instructive campaign that helps the people grow in organization and consciousness, uses the same methods to sell its candidates as the ruling classes do.

564   This means that when the Left suffers an electoral defeat, the campaign leaves behind not only frustration, burn-out and debt; the election effort fails to lead to political growth for those who worked for and supported the campaign, but leaves only a bitter feeling that everything was in vain. The situation would be very different if the campaign were planned from a fundamentally educational-instructional perspective, using it to strengthen consciousness and popular organisation. In that case, even if the results of the election were far from satisfactory, the time and effort invested in the campaign would not be lost.

565   The tendency to adapt to the given milieu not only puts constraints on action; according to Carlos Vilas, it also produces 'internal changes in one's ideological orientation, in the programme proposals, and in the scope of its action'.[264]

General challenges facing the institutional Left

566   The undeniable institutional progress of the Left must not make us forget that the existing set of democratic institutions offers advantages, but also imposes restrictions. As Enriquo Rubio says, the biggest challenge we face is to discover how to 'maximise the former and minimise the latter'. We must also discover how to bring together forces that want change and don't want the existing order – particularly when just by participating in bourgeois institutions we legitimise them to a certain extent – and how to build an 'alternative set of institutions' through the actions of the 'various social and political actors'.[265]

567   Therefore, there are more than a few challenges facing the Left before it can – through the use of existing institutions – successfully accumulate support for change and not for the preservation of the status quo.

How to avoid slipping into traditional political practices

568   One of these challenges is that a big effort must be made to avoid slipping into traditional political practices. This can be done by developing new practices that clearly show the difference between the way popular parties and other political parties operate. This is the only way to win over a public increasingly sceptical of politics and politicians.

569   Second, the Left should avoid slipping into the usual deformations of bourgeois political practice.

570   One of these deformations is *political careerism*, which is the idea that one should always be rising through the ranks, that going back to being a simple rank-and-file party member is a demotion. Often the organisation itself justifies this attitude by arguing that the investment it has made in training cadres should not be wasted.

571   On that subject, the cadre policies implemented in Porto Alegre are interesting. The PT (Workers Party) has now been in office there for three consecutive terms. They have rotated cadres between the administrative apparatus, the party and the popular movement; in this way, the experience acquired in one of these spheres is transferred to the others. This is especially useful in the case of cadres who have acquired administrative experience.

572   Another harmful attitude is that of a preference for '*court circles*' over work with the rank and file. As Lula[266] said, several years after having been elected president of Brazil, there are cadres who 'are seduced by the perfume of the élite and now can't stand the smell of the people'. They often rely on bureaucratic barriers to avoid direct contact with the people and tend to receive their information from groups of advisers, losing the opportunity to take the people's pulse. They seem to be unaware that the strongest cordon of disinformation is created by those who should keep them informed. These 'advisers' have the habit of accentuating the positive and eliminating the negative, either from the noble motive of not wanting to overburden those they advise with worries or from the selfish desire to be congratulated for being the bearers of good news. Another deformation is that of using the party as a trampoline for personal

advancement and the press as a means of self-enhancement and self-promotion – whereas party and press should be tools for ideological struggle against those who oppress the people.

573   Another challenge to cadres is to avoid being co-opted by a system which spreads thousands of nets to catch the unwary. These range from salaries, which are much higher than any representatives of the popular movement can earn from their work, to the series of perks that go with the job: air travel, hotels, expenses, paid advisers and even housing, as well as the social status that such a position brings.

Specific challenges to local government

574   There are a number of specific challenges to local government.

575   Avoid what one Leftist Italian politician called 'state cretinism',[267] the belief that 'the state is a neutral body', that it is 'like an empty bottle that can be filled with any liquid, that it can be used equally to benefit one class or another because its function is merely technical'.

576   It is not about governing for the sake of governing; nor about only administrating a crisis. It is about governing in a different way, showing on a local level what the Left could do nationally. As I said, a good local government is, at a time when there is so much scepticism, the best visiting card the Left has.

577   I agree with Carlos Vilas[268] that one of the greatest challenges the Left faces is how to endow democratic institutions with transformative potential; how to strengthen the value of democracy without legitimising capitalism or abandoning a project of transformation.

578   If, at the municipal level, the Left aspires to be something more than a good administrator of macro-economic policies that are set at other levels of government, then it should be capable of coordinating these local or regional levels with national problems in order to show the population the limits of neo-liberalism.

579   It is not easy for the Latin American Left, accustomed to being the opposition, to suddenly become the government. One of its greatest challenges, according to Tarso Genro,[269] is 'how to succeed in becoming a governing party without ceasing to be a party of struggle'.

580   I agree with Massimo Gorla that the presence of a political group 'in [official] institutions only has a raison d'être as long as it is a reflection of another much more energetic and mass-based opposition: an opposition

of hundreds of thousands of workers who oppose the regime in the streets, who fight it and who, through their struggles, forge an alternative for change. This is the true opposition: the struggle of the masses.'[270]

581   It is necessary to be true to one's democratic beliefs, which means really bestowing decision-making power on the people.

582   The Participatory Budget (as it has come to be known) in the PT-run local governments in Brazil, especially in Porto Alegre, provide a notable example of how the power of deliberation was granted to an organised community. Similar experiments have been made in the Montevideo town government – run by the Frente Amplio of Uruguay – and in the municipalities governed by La Causa R in Venezuela.

583   The people's governments should be completely *transparent* and willing to submit to *public control* over their finances, over the use of state resources and over their employment practices.

584   The *autonomy* of popular organisations must be respected, accepting as normal any tensions and contradictions between the government and the popular movement. That means, among other things, avoiding the tendency to draft leaders from popular movements into the administrative apparatus. It also means accepting and promoting the autonomy of popular movements even if they have positions that conflict with those of the government.

Specific challenges in the election arena

585   The greatest challenge to the Left in this arena is to be capable of fighting any electoralist deviation, which manifests itself in the following traits: (1) *the tendency to make getting elected an end in itself* rather than a means to work on a project of social transformation (this tendency explains why cadres cling to their legislative positions and consider it a humiliation to return to being simple rank-and-file members); (2) linking up with popular movements only during elections and for electoral reasons; (3) individualism during the campaign: seeking funds and support for themselves and not for the party; (4) internal conflicts over the elections, as if the other members of the party were their main enemies, and so on.

586   The Left must fight against the individualist mandates typical of bourgeois politics, which is characterised by the voters' lack of control over the representatives they elect. A mandate should be sacred; it must

respect the will of the voters. Therefore, if for any reason elected representatives leave the political organisation they belonged to when elected, they should resign their seats.

587   An example of the correct attitude in this sense, which was nevertheless described as quixotic, was that of Hugo Cores, leader of the Uruguayan Partido por la Victoria del Pueblo (Party for the People's Victory), who was elected deputy from the list of the Movimiento de Participación Popular coalition (MPP). When he left the coalition he resigned from his post as a member of parliament.

588   For this very reason, one of the political organisation's jobs, which is of equal or perhaps greater importance than that of nominating candidates, is the control it exercises over them once they have been elected.

589   One reason the Left has always had for agreeing to work in bourgeois institutions is that they provide a space from which to circulate the ideas of the Left to more people and reach even the most backward sectors. In other words, to turn parliament into a sounding board, a platform from which to denounce the outrages, abuses, and injustices of a regime based upon oppression. Today, however, the monopolistic control that the ruling classes often exercise over the media creates a veritable *barrier of silence* which gets in the way of this goal and is very difficult to overcome if the Left is not well represented in parliament.

590   Another great challenge facing the Left is *how to get the media to report on what the Left does*. This challenge can only be confronted successfully with great creativity – as the Zapatistas and Greenpeace did – or by creating political events that are impossible to ignore, like the important march of the MST (Brazil's Landless Workers Movement) to the Brazilian capital in 1997 or children painting murals with democratic messages in Caracas, as they did when Aristóbulo Istúriz was mayor.

591   Also of great interest is the successful way the FMLN in El Salvador let the people know what they were doing in parliament by holding open sessions in public squares.

592   The Left must struggle to overcome the enormous influence of the audiovisual media monopolised by the Right. Their messages permeate all of society, especially the poorest and most downtrodden sectors which, as we saw previously, are incapable of establishing a critical distance from them. Many concede defeat, thinking that this battle can only be waged in an arena that is overwhelmingly unfavourable to the Left.

A creative approach to the a-legal

593　Finally, as we've already seen, besides the area of the *legal arena* and its opposite – the illegal arena – there is a whole other arena that we have suggested could be called the *a-legal*, that arena which is neither legal nor illegal. The Left often lacks the creativity to use this space.

594　By moving ahead in the institutional realm, aware of the challenges this presents and creatively taking over the a-legal spaces, the Latin American Left can accumulate forces for change and help bring about people's cultural transformation, making sure that they take more and more responsibility for their own destiny. In doing so, the Left lays the foundations of the new society we want to build – a society where the people are the active subjects at every level.

Chapter 14
The Bolivarian Revolution — Is it a Revolution?

595   In what follows, and to end this book, we shall look at how the questions raised above have been approached in Venezuela.

596   Hugo Chávez, an ex-soldier who was elected president of Venezuela at the end of 1998 after winning the elections by an ample majority, believes he is building a new history. He is trying to make a real revolution by making structural changes in the political, social, moral and economic spheres but is trying to do this peacefully and democratically in order to make the far-reaching, necessary changes viable. Seven and a half years after these these goals were set,[271] can we say that there is a revolutionary process in Venezuela, when the bourgeois state apparatus has not been violently destroyed and there have been no far-reaching economic reforms? Isn't it really a reformist process?

The state takes the initiative in changing the rules of the game and creating spaces for participation

597   Unlike other Left governments in the region, President Chávez was certain before his election victory that unless the rules of the institutional game were changed he could not carry out the far-reaching socio-economic transformations that the country urgently needed. Therefore his first revolutionary initiative was to convene a Constituent Assembly to write a new constitution which would make it possible to create the legal framework of the new, humanist, solidarity-filled society that they had set out to build.

Participation and human development in the Bolivarian Constitution

598   The most striking thing about the Bolivarian Constitution is the emphasis it places on popular participation in public affairs and how it is this protagonism that will ensure the complete development of both individuals and the collective. In Article 20 it states that 'all men and women have the right to the free development of their personality'; in Article 102 it refers to the need to 'develop the creative potential of each human being and the full enjoyment of his or her personality in a democratic society' and in article 299 it speaks of 'ensuring overall human development'. Article 62 indicates the way this development will be achieved. That article says that 'the participation of the people in forming, carrying out and controlling the management of public affairs is the necessary way of achieving the involvement which ensures their complete development, both individual and collective'. It then goes on to say that: 'It is the obligation of the State and the duty of society to facilitate the creation of the conditions most favourable to putting this into practice'.[272] Article 70 lists other ways which allow the people to develop 'their abilities and skills'; these are 'self-management, cooperatives of all kinds, democratic planning, and participatory budgets at all levels of society'.

599   President Chávez and his government have taken the constitution's mandate very seriously and have made every effort to encourage participation at all levels. It is probable that Venezuela is the only country which has a ministry devoted to participation: the Ministry of Popular Participation and Social Development, which was created in mid-2005. One of its principal objectives is to remove obstacles and make it easier for there to be for popular participation from below throughout the country.

The communal councils: local spaces ideal for allowing everyone to participate

600   In the sphere of local, where-you-live participation, emphasis has been put on participatory diagnoses, the participatory budget, and social auditing. Initially local public planning councils (CLPP) were created at the municipal level to carry out these tasks with representatives from

existing institutions (the mayor, town councillors, members of parish boards)[273] and community representatives. It is important to point out that representation is weighted in favour of the communities (51 per cent as against 49 per cent), a clear reflection of the political will to encourage community participation. Practice showed, however, that true people's protagonism could only emerge if participation was encouraged in much smaller spaces. This is how the idea of the communal councils arose.

601 The first question to be resolved was: what was the ideal space for participation when it came to local power?

Families which make up the community

602 A great deal of debate ensued, focused on successful community organising experiences such as the urban land committees (CTU) – each consisting of about 200 families who organise in their struggle to bring some order to land ownership – and the health committees, each of which brings about 150 families together with the aim of supporting the doctors in the worst-off communities. The conclusion was reached that a community had to be understood as a group of families living in a specific geographic area who know each other and can relate easily, who can meet without having to depend on transport, and who have a common history, use the same public services and share similar economic, social and urban development problems. The idea was that there would be 200–400 families in an urban community area and 20–50 in a rural area.

603 The number of people in a community varies greatly from one place to another. The conclusion reached was that in a densely populated urban area, where there are housing developments and boroughs with tens of thousands of inhabitants, the number of people in a community can vary from one to two thousand people, whereas in an isolated rural area, where communities are small hamlets, the number ranges from 100 and 250 people.

604 Making an approximate calculation, in Venezuela, which has around 26 million inhabitants, there could be about 52,000 communities.

605 Each of these communities has to elect a body which will act as the community government. This body is called the communal council.

Coordinating all community efforts into a single plan

606   When the communal councils are set up the specific characteristics of each community must be taken into account. There are some communities that have strong traditions of organising and struggle and therefore already have different sorts of community organisations within their borders. There are others that may have one or two and yet others with none. The organisations that might be found in a community in Venezuela include: the urban land committee, the protection committee, the health committee and the community health organisation, cultural groups, the sports club, the residents' association, the educational missions, the technical water board, the energy board, the Bolivarian circle, environmental groups, food committees, the OAPs club, the community housing organisation, the popular defence unit, cooperatives, micro-companies, and the people's economy council, and more. Each of these organisations has a tendency to 'do its own thing'.

607   The tasks of each specific area must be taken on collectively by the various organisations that are identified with this particular matter. The Overall Social Development collective, let's say, must bring together, for example, the Social Protection Committee, the Health Committee, and the Food Organisations that exist in the community and other types of organisation that can work with them in the struggle to ensure the health and quality of life of everyone (in the community) and especially of those who live in extreme poverty.

608   It is not a case, therefore, of wiping the slate clean in those places where the community is already organised; on the contrary, what needs to be done is to coordinate all existing initiatives into a single work plan. Working as a whole and not in different areas, as was done before, makes it possible to obtain much better results and to avoid duplicating efforts.

609   Drawing up this single plan is another of the communal council's tasks. It must be based on a participative diagnosis through which the community makes the problems that it can solve with its own material and human resources a priority. Setting goals that are possible to achieve with the active help of as many members of the community as possible means that results are seen very quickly and this increases the community's self-esteem and makes them even more motivated to participate. If the diagnosis is not made using a participative diagnosis, what usually happens

is that instead of encouraging participation, the community stands around doing nothing waiting for the state to solve the problems identified.

610   If it happens that the amount of money needed or the complexity of the problem is beyond the community's means, the communal council must draw up projects to present to the participatory budget or to other financing bodies and make certain all necessary arrangements have been made for receiving the funding that may be allocated. The participatory budget process became infinitely richer once the communal councils were in existence because it is they who set the priorities in much smaller assemblies where citizen participation is more complete. The idea is that the spokespersons for the communal councils and the residents of these communities should take an active part in the participatory budget.

611   Finally, and mentioning only their most important functions, the communal councils must encourage the collective to act as a financial watchdog over all activities undertaken in the community, whether these are carried out by the state, the community or by private companies (food, education, health, culture, sports, infrastructure, cooperatives, missions, etcetera). It also manages the moneys given to it or which it obtains through its own initiative.

'Voceros' and the citizens' assembly

612   So that these the communal councils could carry out their mandate it was thought that they should have an executive subcommittee, an auditing subcommittee and a finance subcommittee.

613   Once problems are identified and work areas defined, the community has to elect those residents who — because of their leadership, knowledge of the field, community work spirit, willingness to work collectively, honour and dynamism — are the best people to represent them on the communal council.

614   Spokespersons for each work area, for the social financial watchdog subcommittee and for the finance subcommittee must be elected.

615   Those who analyse, discuss, decide and elect their spokespersons in a citizens' assembly are the people who live in that geographic area. An effort must be made to see that at least one member of every family comes to these meetings, The Communal Councils Act, passed on 9 April 2006 after a national debate, set quorums at 10 per cent of the population of any community over the age of 15. There were many who suggested

lowering the minimum age to 12, since children of around that age are often the most willing to cooperate in community-type work. They are not burdened down by the apathy that previous broken promises have engendered in those older than they. Moreover, filling their leisure time with this kind of activity might be a good antidote to the danger of drugs and bad company.

616   The citizens' assembly is the highest authority in the community. Its decisions are binding on the communal council. *It is there that the people's sovereignty and power reside.*

617   Those elected to be part of the communal council are called *voceros* because they are the community's voice. Therefore, when their fellow residents lose confidence in them because they have ceased to transmit what the community thinks and decides to the communal council, these people have to be recalled, they can no longer be the community's voice. Venezuelan militants refuse to use the word 'representative' because of the negative connotations that this word has acquired in the bourgeois representative system. Candidates only come to the communities at election time, promise everything under the sun, and then are never seen again after the elections.

Respecting the community's maturation process

618   In addition, it should be made clear that setting up a communal council is not something that happens overnight. It requires a process of community maturation. Therefore the proposal was made to form a provisional organising team elected by the community in an assembly. This team's most important job would be to prepare the way for the residents to elect the members of the communal council with full knowledge of the issues at hand. This team would have to make a socio-economic study of the community by visiting the families house by house, and would have to arrange for a community participatory diagnosis to identify the main problems. The hope is that by making this team responsible for these jobs, the potential future members of the communal council get a good foundation, that they learn all about the problems in their community after their dedication to that community and their reliability has been tested in practice. According to how they perform, all the members of the organising team, or maybe just some of them, will be elected spokes-persons for the communal council.

619   It has been stressed repeatedly that any type of manipulation, political or other, must be avoided when setting up the communal councils. This means councils do not have to be Chavist communal councils: these community institutions are open to all citizens, no matter what their political stripe. It would not be surprising if, after fighting to solve community problems and when they see how much support they receive from the government, many of these people who have had the wool pulled over their eyes by the media discover what the true Bolivarian revolutionary project is.

620   I have absolutely no doubt that the communal councils are one of the spaces that will make a huge contribution to the full development of human beings and are a solid basis on which socialism for the twenty-first century can be built.

Encouraging worker participation

621   The role of the Bolivarian government has been crucial both for developing local participation and for the participatory process that is taking place in the production sphere. People have been encouraged to form cooperatives. In March 2004 an ambitious programme, Mision Vuelvan Caras, was set in motion. It began by recruiting a million people from the educational missions. The idea was not just to give them a job but to bring about Venezuela's economic, political and cultural transformation by focusing on endogenous development.

622   Vuelvan Caras not only offered credit but also gave emphasis to preparing people for the new relations of production by giving classes in cooperation and self-management. There were only 762 cooperatives when Chávez was elected for the first time in 1998 but by 2005 there were already almost 84,000, and almost a million cooperative members.

623   More recently there has been a move towards creating social production companies which are guided not by the logic of capital but by a humanist, solidarity-based logic. And there have been attempts, although in my opinion somewhat timid ones, to implement self-management in some strategic state companies.

624   Whenever I think about an economy that is an alternative to capitalism I remember that once, a number of years ago, I heard Fidel Castro say in the National Assembly of People's Power that socialism still had not

managed to find a way to motivate production that replaced the capitalist whip.

625   Dario Machado, a Cuban researcher, has suggested that in the experience of socialism in Eastern Europe 'the workers never reached the point of feeling that they were the owners of the means of production and services'; they were the '*de jure* owners' but there was no participatory management to match this. Whereas they did the work, others above decided 'what to produce and how to do it'.[274]

626   When I read over what he said, I wonder if the answer to the question President Castro asked isn't contained therein.

627   In Venezuela, long before Chávez suggested that the Bolivarian Revolution had to go down the road to socialism, and before anyone had been legally given ownership of any company, a group of workers in a strategic area of the economy had begun to feel that they were the owners of their company. It was at the time of the oil strike and sabotage: the opposition thought that if around 18,000 managers and specialist workers from the state-owned company PDVSA withdrew their labour, the productive lungs of the country would collapse, causing chaos, and this would allow them to get rid of Chávez. However, the rank-and-file oil company workers turned up *en masse* to work and many retired technicians offered their services to the company. They worked tirelessly, often with no boss, motivated by their patriotic consciousness; they felt proud of and responsible for what went on; they used the knowledge they had obtained through daily practice and they invented innovative solutions. At that point, work collectives began to form in which all strata of company workers took part, from the chief engineer and the foreman down to the shopfloor workers. Their aim, once production had been normalised, was to rethink the company, restructure it, and eliminate nests of corruption: to eliminate privileges and give subcontracted work to cooperatives instead of private companies.

628   The electricity workers also began to feel that same sense of ownership. Aware that the electricity company CADAFE was one of the opposition's targets, they organised to prevent any attempt to sabotage it. Before the military coup and as a way of struggling to put the company back on its feet – it had been practically dismantled by management in order to provide a justification for privatisation – the CADAFE workers had begun to raise the question of co-management. This was the outcome

of a long struggle against the privatisation of the company, which had been proposed by previous governments.

629   As a way of giving recognition to the workers' noble, patriotic attitude during the attempted opposition strike, President Chávez decreed that two union leaders be made members of the boards of directors of both companies. This measure was taken without consulting the workers of the aforementioned companies.

630   Unfortunately, some of those union leaders stuck to practices from past eras: self-interested behaviour, charging people a commission for giving them a job, and so on. This, plus the fact that many managers felt threatened when they had to face a group of organised workers demanding transparency and questioning their management, provided the arguments which began to convince some government members, including President Chávez, that there could be no co-management in strategic companies. The risk could not be taken that the workers might, because of their lack of political maturity, run the company to satisfy their group interests while forgetting about the rest of society.

631   At first sight this seems like a convincing argument. Nevertheless, the argument put forward by Carlos Sánchez, the president of CADELA, a CADAFE affiliate in the Andean region, seems to us to be even more convincing. He said that 'in order for co-management in a company as strategically important as the electricity company to meet the noble aims of serving the country, and not be detoured into serving petty personal interests, or the interests of political parties, social or union groups, it is essential that the actors of co-management include the organised community as well as the company's workers because, when all is said and done, the electricity company does not belong to the electricity workers, it belongs to all Venezuelans and the voice of these Venezuelans must be transmitted to the company through the communities which receive its services and they should have a voice so they can point out the deficiencies in those services, suggest solutions and collaborate in their implementation.'[275]

632   In Mérida State this type of co-management has been implemented with excellent results. Services have improved markedly. The electricity workers, who were previously given the cold shoulder by the community because of the poor service the company provided, are today welcomed with affection: payment of bills has increased enormously and the number

of homes 'stealing' electricity has been greatly reduced. The explanation for these results can be found in a zone manager proposed by the workers, a general manager who was capable of backing this decision, a union leader (a woman) who got on really well with the workers and worked in harmony with the manager, and meetings with workers and communities to discuss how to do things better.

633   What it comes down to is that responsibility is shared between all the parties. However, in order for this to be viable the workers have to trust those who manage the company because, as the president of the Federación Electrica Angel Navas said, if this trust is not there, workers will not commit themselves. 'How are we going to agree to share the responsibility if we see that we have no means to avoid all the bad stuff that happens?'

634   Navas then explained what co-management means for the workers: 'It allows them to find things out, to be able to participate. In 19 years they never once came down here to ask me what my opinion was on how the work should be done. The company executives would send me some memos saying: "Look, you should do this and this and this." If workers' opinions start to be taken into account, workers grow; they develop through their work. People are creators, they are transformers. If people are overlooked at work they die. If workers feel useless, if they are not allowed to express their creativity, if they are constantly told "No, you can't do that!" if all there is, is an antagonistic clash all the time, at the end all you have is a bunch of frustrated people. It is different when the workers feel that their opinions are being listened to, when there is communication. That's the crux of co-management.'

635   'When we talk of co-management we are talking about a cohesion between everyone to make the company more efficient and more productive, to socialise the company to the country.'

636   'We have to fight for that, and it is the state itself that should be the most interested in this because what we workers do with this mechanism, if we stop to take stock, is that we self-exploit ourselves more, don't we? Yes, but now we enjoy it! For years now I have been working three or sometimes four times as much as I did before! But now I am satisfied doing so. Before I used to work for the goods they paid me for something I did; now I do it with all my heart. That is the transformation that takes place in the workers: they change spiritually, they are less bothered about

material things than about feeling useful, their satisfaction is feeling that they are doing something for their community.'[276]

637   Angel Navas's testimony shows the fundamental part that co-management can play in strategic state industries; it not only benefits the workers but also benefits the society. It lets us see how the fact of being listened to, of being able to take part in taking the decisions about what has to be done in the company, is the most important incentive the workers have to put the best of themselves into their work. It liberates productive forces. Work ceases to be alienating. It transforms the workers spiritually, makes them feel useful and part of a much bigger family than their own company. It allows them to reach a higher level of self-development.

The state from a revolutionary perspective

638   The above information and thoughts show us how important it is that Left forces struggle to take over state power so they can direct the state apparatus from a revolutionary perspective. Although it may seem contradictory to some, it is possible, from above, to encourage people to build democratic power from below. What cannot be done is to decree democracy from above, because democracy requires that a cultural transformation take place in people. But it is possible to create more and more spaces — and these *must* be created — where the people can participate as active subjects in the practice which produces the required cultural transformation.

639   Fighting for a democracy from below in communities and where people work should be the task of those who are committed to the struggle for an alternative, socialist society, if we clearly understand that, as Michael Lebowitz says, socialism is the path; the aim is the full development of human beings.[277]

On the political instrument that could move these ideas forward

640   But what kind of political instrument could move these ideas forward? Perhaps some lessons can be drawn from the kind of organisation that resulted in the categorical triumph of the No vote in the August 2005

referendum which the opposition had called to try to end President Chávez's term in office. Some people advised Chávez to refuse to allow the referendum on the grounds of fraud. But Chávez decided to defeat the opposition through democracy – protagonistic democracy.

A leap forward in things organisational

641   Since he was well aware of the weaknesses of the political parties that supported him, Chávez could not rely on them to provide the leadership that would win this decisive electoral battle in which the future of the revolutionary project was at stake. The president decided to invent a mechanism to organise the electoral campaign through direct reliance on his followers. He recognised that people wanted to support him but did not have an appropriate mechanism. That is how the idea arose of creating small groups of activists or electoral patrols throughout the country. These units were formed of groups of 10 political or social activists (militants) and their most important job was to 'work' 10 more people each by going door to door, trying to get as many of these people as possible to commit to voting against the recall: in other words, to commit to voting No. Each patrol, therefore, was responsible for 'working' 100 electors and if the constituency had 2,000 registered voters, for example, 20 patrols had to be created, that is, 200 patrol members had to be organised and they had to divide the work on 2,000 electors between them. Chávez's original idea was that no family would be left unvisited. Chávez called upon the people to organise themselves, and the people responded with incredible enthusiasm and energy.

642   Although many of them did not meet all the requirements set forth by Chávez, this type of organisation meant that hundreds of thousands of sympathisers were able to work on a concrete political task, whether there was or was not any party campaigning in their geographical area. Many people who were emotionally committed to the Bolivarian Revolution, but who had been inactive until then, had their first political, organising experience. Many anonymous people did their bit, as did those government members who were able to put aside their personal and departmental projects and who decided to work closely with the rank and file with just one aim in mind: that the 'No's should win.

643   The Venezuelan people came out of this practical experience greatly strengthened. Their self-esteem grew, and they grew as human beings.

More than an electoral victory, quantitative, it was a moral victory, qualitative.

644   This experience showed that it was possible to overcome the organic dispersal of the immense activist potential that existed in the country by creating a meeting space for all those willing to fight for a common aim: keeping their president at the helm of the nation, whether or not they were or were not members of a given political or social organisation. A type of organisation which went far beyond the sum of political parties and popular social organisations was created. This made it possible to undertake a wide variety of initiatives to achieve the goal. Some people worked when they got home from work, others during the day; some took campaign literature, for others the best campaign literature was their own personal history: the joy of learning to read, a child saved by a Cuban doctor.

645   Returning to my initial question, can we say that there is no revolutionary process in Venezuela when the popular sectors are transforming themselves into the true protagonists of history in that process and the government is creating the foundations for a new state that is built from below?

646   In an era of neo-liberal globalisation, this is the best way of contributing to the struggle against powerful enemies who oppose the humanist, solidarity-filled, socialist world we want to build.

Notes

1 Juan Antonio Blanco, *El Tercer Milenio, una visión alternativa de la post modernidad* (Havana, Cuba: Centro Félix Varela, 1995), p. 117.

2 The present work owes particular debts to *La izquierda en el umbral de Siglo XXI. Haciendo posible lo imposible* (Mexico City and Madrid): Siglo XXI and Siglo XXI de España, 1999) (translated into French, Italian and Portugese); *La izquierda después de Seattle* (Madrid): Siglo XXI, de España, 2002); 'Acerca del sujeto político capaz de responder a los desafíos del siglo XXI', paper given at the International Conference on 'Karl Marx and the Challenges of the Twenty-First Century', Havana, 5–10 May 2003; 'On Leftist Strategy', *Science and Society*, 69, 2 (April 2005); *Venezuela, Una revolución sui generis*, Caracas: Ministerio of Culture Press, 2004.

3 Not counting the interviews I did when I was editor of the political weekly *Chile HOY* (1971–3), I have interviewed forty top-level Left leaders, and more than a hundred second-level leadership cadres. The first group includes President Hugo Chávez of Venezuela; the president of Bolivia, Evo Morales; the president of Brazil, Luis Ignacio da Silva, the president of Uruguay, Tabaré Vásquez; the five FMLN comandantes and two of the top leaders of the Convergencia Democratica (El Salvador); the three comandantes of URNG (Guatemala); six of the nine Sandinista comandantes (Nicaragua); four of the five comandantes of the Coordinadora Guerrillera Simón Bolívar, as well as the presidents of the political fronts Unión Patriotica and A Luchar (Colombia); the president of the Brazilian Workers Party (PT) and five PT mayors; the Montevideo mayor, a member of the Uruguayan Frente Amplio; two mayors from La Causa R (Venezuela) and its secretary general; general secretaries from Uruguayan and Peruvian parties; and three top-level Cuban leaders. I have also found the writings of the following comrades to be very useful: those of Enrique Rubio (1991, 1994) leader of Vertiente Artiguista and deputy in the Uruguayan parliament; those of Clodomiro Almeyda (1991–97) the recently deceased Chilean socialist leader who was Salvador Allende's foreign minister; Carlos Ruíz a sociologist and university professor from Chile, and Franz Hinkelammert, a German economist and theologian.

4 The use of microcomputers in the control unit of machines. Discovered in the 1950s, microcomputers went into production in the 1970s. See Eduardo Viera, *Fin de Siglo: la crisis estructural del capitalismo* (Montevideo: Talleres Gráficos de Punto Sur, 1997), p. 64.

5 Carlota Pérez, 'Las nuevas tecnologías: una vision de conjunto', in *La tercera revolución industrial (impactos internacionales del actual viraje tecnológico)* (Buenos Aires: RIAL, 1986), p. 79.

6 Jeremy Rifkin, *The End of Work: The Decline of the Global Labour Force and the Dawn of the Post-Market Era* (New York: Putnam, 1996), p. 154.

7 Manuel Castells, *The Information Age: Economy, Society and Culture. Volume 1: The Rise of the Network Society* (Oxford, Blackwell, 1996), p. 120.

8 Especially in Europe. See F. Chesnais, 'Notas para una caracterización', *Carré Rouge* (Paris, October–December 1996).

9 William I. Robinson, 'A Case Study of Globalization Processes in the Third World: a

Transnational Agenda in Nicaragua,' *Global Society* 11, 1 (1996): 61–91. R. Agacino, *La anatomía de la globalización y de la intergración económica*, mimeographed document. Stgo de Chile, 1997, p. 9. See also Octavio Ianni, 'La internacionalización del capital', *Teorías de la globalización*, Mexico City, Siglo XXI (1999), pp. 31–43.

10   W. I. Robinson, 'A Case Study...', p. 200. I say 'in those places' because they could indeed become veritable enclaves.

11   R. Reich, *The Work of Nations*: *Preparing Ourselves for Twenty-First Century Capitalism* (London: Simon and Schuster, 1991), pp. 110–88.

12   *Ibid.*, pp. 113–14.

13   *Ibid.,* pp. 110–88.

14   *Ibid.*, pp. 110–11.

15   *Ibid.*, p. 112.

16   *Ibid.*, p. 171.

17   See Neil Reynolds, 'US Trade Deficit Is an All in the Family Affair', *Globe and Mail*, 22 February 2006.

18   Peter F. Drucker, 'Trading Places', *The National Interest,* Spring 2005.

19   *Ibid.*

20   Peter Drucker, *Post Capitalist Society* (New York: HarperCollins, 1993), pp. 1–17.

21   On this topic, see Juan Antonio Blanco's book, *Tercer Milenio* (note 1).

22   Several authors, including, for example, Carlota Pérez, recognise five technological revolutions, the first coinciding with the industrial revolution in the final decades of the eighteenth century with the latest one happening now. See Pérez, 'Las nuevas tecnologías', pp. 43–89.

23   Alvin Toffler, *The Third Wave* (New York: Random House, 1987), pp. 19–20.

24   Pedro Monreal, 'Tecnología Flexible y crisis económica: el caso de las industria norteamericana en las década de los ochenta', doctoral thesis, Centro de Investigación de la Economía Internacional, University of Havana, Cuba, 1998.

25   R. Agacino, 'La anatomía', p. 15.

26   N. Chomsky, 'La Sociedad global', in *Globalización, exclusión y democracia en América Latina* (Mexico City: Ed. Contrapuntos/Joaquín Mortiz, 1997), p. 13.

27   E. Hobsbawm, *The Age of Extremes: the Short Twentieth Century, 1914–1991* (London: Michael Joseph, 1994).

28   Michael Hardt and Antonio Negri, *Multitude* (New York: Penguin, 2004).

29   Leo Panitch, 'Globalización, estados y estrategias de Izquierda', in P. González Casanova and J. F. Saxe-Fernández (eds), *El mundo actual: situación y alternativas*, Siglo XXI (Mexico City, 1996), p. 92.

30   Carlos Ruiz, 'Reconstrucción del movimiento popular y luchas de poder', *Surda*, 11 (Santiago de Chile, December 1996) p. 4.

31   Franz Hinkelammert, 'Nuestro proyecto de nueva sociedad en América Latina: el papel regulador del estado y los problemas de autorregulación del mercado', in *Cultura de la esperanza y sociedad sin exclusión* (San Jose de Costa Rica: Ed. DEI, 1995), p. 114.

32   Martín Hernández, 'Las democracias protegidas y la dominación democrática del capital financiero', in *Revista de Ciencias Sociales (Trabajo y Capital)*, (Uruguay, November 1989), p.146.

33   Germán Sánchez, 'Problemas de la democracia en nuestra América', in *Revolución y Democracia* (Llallagua, Bolivia: National University, Siglo XX, 1992), p. 25.

34   Martín Hernández, 'Las democracias protegidas', pp. 146–7.

35   *Ibid.*, p.142.
36   Martín Hernández's expression.
37   *Ibid.*, p. 144.
38   Carlos Ruiz, 'Democracia y relaciones laborales. Una visión desde la transformación del mundo de la industria en Chile', degree dissertation, Sociology Department, University of Chile, Santiago, October 1996, p. 90.
39   H. Gallardo, 'Democratización y democracia en América Latina', paper given in Buenos Aires, October 1996, p. 13.
40   M. Hernández, 'Las democracias protegidas', p.151.
41   See the study of eight local popular participation governments in Marta Harnecker, *Haciendo camino al andar* (Santiago de Chile: LOM/MEPLA, 1995).
42   Tomás Moulián, 'Capitalismo, democracia y campo cultural en Chile', *Encuentro*, 21, 2 (May 1995), p. 35.
43   *Ibid.*
44   Jeremy Rifkin, *The End of Work. The Decline of the Global Labour Force and the Dawn of the Post-Market Era* (New York: Tarcher/Putnam, 1995), pp. 41–2.
45   *Ibid.*
46   *Ibid.*, p. 42.
47   *Ibid.*, p. 43.
48   *Ibid.*, p. 45.
49   T. Moulián, *Chile actual, anatomia de un mito* (Santiago de Chile: Ed Arcis/LOM, 1997), p. 105.
50   *Ibid.*, p. 121.
51   T. Moulián, 'Capitalismo, democracia' (note 42). pp. 36.
52   *Ibid.*
53   Ignacio Ramonet, *Un mundo sin rumbo (Crisis de fin de siglo)* (Madrid: Ed. Debate, 1997), p. 213.
54   *Ibid.*, pp. 221–2.
55   Paul Virilio, 'Peligros, riesgos y amenazas', in *Cine Cubano*, 142 (special issue, Havana. 1998), 'Dossier: Ante la globalización del nuevo milenio: todavía la utopía', p. 32.
56   Eric Hobsbawm, *The Age of Extremes* (note 27), p. 22.
57   Umberto Eco quoted in Enrique Rubio and Marcelo Pereira, *Utopía y estrategia, democracia y socialismo* (Montevideo, Uruguay: Ed. Trilce, 1994), p. 64.
58   Juan Antonio Blanco, *El Tercer Milenio*, speaks of 'the postmodern opiate of the oppressed', p. 117.
59   Eduardo Galeano, 'Hacia una sociedad de la incomunicación', in *Cine Cubano* 142 (special issue, Havana, 1998), 'Dossier: Ante la globalización del nuevo milenio: todavía la utopía', p. 17.
60   So-called world culture. I. Ramonet, *Un mundo sin rumbo*, p. 63.
61   José Joaquín Brünner, *Globalización Cultural y Postmodernidad* (Santiago de Chile: Ed. Fondo de Cultura Económica (Brevarios), 1998), p. 151.
62   Benjamin R. Barber, 'Vers une société universelle de consommateurs: Culture McWorld contre démocratie', *Le Monde Diplomatique* (August 1998), p. 14.
63   *Ibid.*, p. 15.
64   Herbert Marcuse, *One Dimensional Man: Studies in the Ideology of Advanced Industrial Society* (Boston: Beacon Press, 1964).
65   For more on this subject read Noam Chomsky's excellent work *Los guardianes de la libertad*

(Barcelona: Ed. Crítica, 1990) and *Necessary Illusions (Thought Control in Democratic Societies)* (London: Pluto Press, 1989).

66   Noam Chomsky, *Necessary Illusions*.

67   José Martí, 'Nuestra América', in *Obras Completas* (Havana: Editorial Nacional de Cuba, 1963–73), Vol. 6, p. 18.

68   Abel Prieto, 'La cigarra y la hormiga: un remake al final del milenio', in *La Gaceta de Cuba*, 1 (January–February 1997), p. 54.

69   Noam Chomsky, 'El control de los medios de comunicación', in *Cómo nos venden la moto* (Barcelona: Ed. Icaria, 1996), pp. 30–1.

70   Carlos Vilas, 'La izquierda en América latina: presente y futuro (notes for a discussion)' in H. Dillas, M. Monereo, J. Valdes Paz (eds), in *Alternativas al neoliberalism* (Madrid, FIMCEA, 1996), p. 42.

71   Alberto Binder, 'La sociedad fragmentada', *Pasos*, Special Issue 3 (1992), pp. 22–6.

72   Marta Harnecker, 'Contra el terrorismo y contra la guerra', in *PUCVIVA* (Brazil, 6 January 2002).

73   Henri Alleg, 'Entretien sur les attentats aux États-Unis et la guerre en Afganistán', in *L'empire en guerre. Le monde après le 11 septembre*, (Paris: Les Temps des Cerises, November 2001), p. 125.

74   Samir Amin, 'Les attentats du 11 septembre', in *L'empire en guerre. Le monde après le 11 septembre*, p. 49.

75   François Chesnais, 'Nous sommes en face de deux ennemis, nous devons reconstruire une perspective internationaliste', in *L'empire en guerre, p.* 161.

76   Henri Alleg, 'Entretien sur les attentats', p. 126.

77   Miguel Urbano Rodrígues, 'O terrorismo de estado norteamericano e o perigo de dictadura militar planetaria', paper for the international seminar 'No to War' at the 2nd World Social Forum Porto Alegre, 2 February 2002.

78   Samir Amin, 'Les attentats du 11 septembre', p. 49.

79   Michel Collon, 'La guerre global a comencé', in *L'empire en guerre – le monde après le 11 septembre* (Paris: Les Temps des Cerises/EPO, 2001).

80   *Ibid.*

81   Noam Chomsky, 'La última desaparición de las fronteras', interview given to Jim Cason and David Brooks, in *La Jornada* newspaper's Sunday supplement, *Masiosare*, Mexico City, February 1998.

82   M. Castells, *The Information Age* (note 7), p. 159.

83   M. Chossudovsky, *The Globalisation of World Poverty: Impacts of the IMF and World Bank Reforms* (London: Zed Books, 1997).

84   Wim Dierckxsens, *Los límites de un capitalismo sin ciudadanía* (San José de Costa Rica: DEI, 1997), p. 140.

85   I. Ramonet, *Un mundo sin rumbo* (note 53), p. 13.

86   Non-commissioned officers and rank-and-file soldiers.

87   Vertiente Artiguista, 'De primera fuerza a gobierno nacional. Perspectivas estratégicas propuestas para el período'. Final version of document No. 5 presented at the Reflection Encounters organised by the Vetiente Artiguista in Maldonado, 28–29 October 2000.

88   Michael Hardt and Antonio Negri, *Multitude* (note 28), p. 215.

89   *Ibid.*, p. 215.

90   *Ibid.*, p. 218.

91   Hugo Cores, notes he made when reading this book, 9 August 2001.

92   Michael Hardt and Antonio Negri, *Multitude*.

93   Helio Gallardo, *El fundamento social de la esperanza* (Quito: Escuela de Formación de Laicos y Laicas, Vicaria Sur de Quito, 1998), p. 6.

94   Vertiente Artiguista, 'De primera fuerza' (note 87).

95   Carlos Ruíz, 'Un proyecto político para los nuevos tiempos', Revista Rebelión Internet. This paper was given at a seminar in the Instituto Paulo Freire, Santiago de Chile, 13 January 2001.

96   *Ibid.*

97   Noam Chomsky, 'El control de los medios de comunicación', in *Cómo se vende la moto* (Barcelona: Editorial Icaria, 1996), p. 16.

98   Carlos Ruíz, 'Un projecto politico'. Many of the ideas I develop below come from his work.

99   *Ibid.*

100 Vertiente Artiguista, 'De primera fuerza' (note 87).

101 *Ibid.*

102 Two particularly important ones are those of Mariátegui in the 1920s and the unfinished attempts of Che Guevara who began to develop his theory of dependence in the 1960s. Others include the contributions of Brazilian researchers Caio Prado junior and Florestan Fernandes.

103 On this, see José Aricó's book, *Marx y América Latina* (Buenos Aires: Catálogos Editora, 1988).

104 An exception is the work of French researcher Charles Bettelheim, who has dedicated more than forty years to this subject.

105 Special mention should be made of Manuel Castells' book, *The Information Age: Network Society* (note 7). On the situation of Western Marxism, see Perry Anderson, *In the Tracks of Historical Materialism* (London: Verso, 1983).

106 C. Almeyda, 'Sobre la dimensión orgánica de la crisis de los partidos de izquierda tradicionales', in *Cuadernos de El Avión Rojo* 5 (Santiago de Chile, winter 1997), p. 14.

107 François Chesnais, 'Propuestas para un trabajo colectivo de renovación programática', *Carré Rouge*, 15–16 (Nov. 2000).

108 Vertiente Artiguista, 'De primera fuerza' (note 87), p. 8.

109 Franz Hinkelammert, 'La lógica de la exclusión del mercado capitalista mundial y el proyecto de liberación', in *Cultura de la esperanza y sociedad sin exclusión* (San José de Costa Rica: DEI, 1995), p. 145.

110 *Ibid.*, p. 147.

111 Hardt and Negri, *Multitude* (note 28), p. 219.

112 Mario Unda, 'El arco iris muestra el país que los poderosos no quieren ver', in *Por el camino del arco iris. Ensayos y testimonios* (Quito, August 1996), pp. 71–2.

113 V. Forrester, *The Economic Horror* (Cambridge: Blackwell, 1999), p. 36.

114 C. Almeyda, 'Sobre la dimensión orgánica' (note 106), p. 13.

115 Hardt and Negri, *Multitude* (note 28), p. 219.

116 Eric Hobsbawm, *The Age of Extremes* (note 27, p. 76).

117 'Thesis on the Structure, Methods and Action of Communist Parties', in Alan Adler (ed.), *Theses, Resolutions and Manifestos of the First Four Congresses of the Third International*, Part II (London: Ink Links, 1983, MIA edition).

118 There is a more detailed analysis of this subject in Marta Harnecker, *Estudiantes, cristianos e indígenas en la revolución* (Mexico City: Siglo XXI, 1987), pp.178–218.

119   Marta Harnecker, 'Los cristianos y la revolución sandinista', interview with Luis Carrión, member of the FSLN national leadership, in *Estudiantes, cristianos e indígenas* (Mexico City: Siglo XXI, 1987), Chapter 11, p. 200.

120   See Marta Harnecker, *Estudiantes, cristianos e indígenas*, Chapter 9, pp. 178–218.

121   See Marta Harnecker, *Estudiantes, cristianos e indígenas*, Chapter 10, pp. 163–77.

122   V. I. Lenin, *Marxism and the State* (Moscow: Progress Publishers, 1980), p. 28.

123   A considerable part of the ideas I expound below were developed in my earlier books: *Vanguardia y crisis actual* (Santiago de Chile: Brecha Editores, 1990), *Hacia el siglo XXI: la izquierda se renueva* (Quito: Ed. Ceesal, 1991).

124   V. I. Lenin, 'The Role and Function of Trade Unions under the New Economic Policy', in V. I. Lenin, *Collected Works* (Moscow: Foreign Languages Publishing House, 1961), Volume 33, pp. 186–7.

125   Mexico City and Madrid: Siglo XXI: 1969, corrected for the third time 1985, 62 editions in Spanish, Portuguese and French.

126   Santiago de Chile: Editorial Quimantú, November 1972.

127   See Louis Althusser, 'Ideology and Ideological State Apparatuses', in *Lenin and Philosophy and other Essays* (London: New Left Books, 1977); and 'Philosophy as a Revolutionary Weapon', *New Left Review*, 1 (64).

128   V. I. Lenin, *What Is To Be Done?* in *Collected Works*, Vol. 5 (Moscow: Foreign Languages Publishing House, 1961), p. 439.

129   *Ibid.*, p. 467.

130   Lenin, *New Tasks and New Forces* (23 February 1905), *Collected Works*. vol. 8, p. 223.

131   Lenin, *Lessons of the Revolution* (6 September 1917), *Collected Works*. vol. 26, p. 309.

132   Lenin, *Collected Works*, vol. 16. p. 440.

133   This way of seeing things excludes a simplified separation and opposition of the economic struggle and the political struggle.

134   Marx, *The Poverty of Philosophy* (New York: International Publishers, 1963).

135   Friedrich Engels, *Letter to Florence Kelley-Wischnewetzky*, London, 28 December 1886, in *Collected Works* (Moscow: Progress Publishers, 1974), vol. 3, pp. 509–10.

136   Marx and Engels to Bebel, W. Leibknecht, W. Bracke and others, 'Circular letter about the manifesto of the Zurichers' (the letter deals with the work of Hoechberg, Berstein and Schram). Marx and Engels sum up the thought of those three in this way: 'the working class is incapable of liberating itself through its own efforts. In order to do so it must place itself under the thumb of educated, propertied members of the bourgeoisie who are the only ones who have the time and opportunity of studying in depth what could be of use to the workers.' K. Marx and F. Engels, *Selected Correspondence* (Moscow: Progress Publishers, 1975).

137   Adolfo Sánchez Vázquez, *Ciencia y revolución. El marxismo de Althusser* (Madrid: Alianza Editorial, 1978), p. 42.

138   Rosa Luxemburg, *The Mass Strike, the Political Party and the Trade Unions* (New York: Harper and Row, 1971).

139   Michael Lebowitz, *Beyond Capital*, second edition (New York: Palgrave Macmillan, 2003) p. 180.

140   Roberto Pittaluga, 'Reflexiones en torno a la idea de espontaneidad en Rosa Luxemburg', in *El Rodaballo*, 5, 9 (1998–9).

141   Karl Marx, *Grundrisse* (Outlines of the Critique of Political Economy) (New York: Penguin, 1973).

142 Adolfo SánchezVázquez, *Ciencia y revolución*, p. 42.

143 *Ibid.*, p. 35.

144 Rosa Luxemburg, *The Mass Strike*, p. 77.

145 Although it needs a class position in order to be a science. This is something we cannot go into here.

146 Louis Althusser criticises this 'absolute verticalism' in *Ce qui ne peut pas durer dans le Parti Communiste Français* (Paris: Maspero, 1978), p. 82.

147 *Ibid.*, p. 69.

148 I want to make it clear that I am not against this type of activity. Quite the contrary, I think that one of the shortcomings of many Left organisations today is having completely neglected these tasks. The question is whether they become an end in themselves or are part of a tactic that gives priority to the people's struggles.

149 Carlos Vilas, 'Democracia y alternativas al neoliberalismo', in *Papers of the FIM No.8 (Alternatives to Development)* (Madrid: Ed. FIM, 1997), p. 34.

150 On this subject of alternatives and the real art of politics and against the idea of politics as *realpolitik* I have been inspired by Franz Hinkelammert. See 'La lógica de la exclusión' (note 109), pp. 151–5.

151 *Ibid.*, p. 153.

152 Gramsci here is thinking of a new correlation of forces.

153 Antonio Gramsci, *Maquiavelo y Lenin*, Ed Popular Nascimento (Santiago de Chile, 1971), pp.78–9.

154 F. Hinkelammert, 'La lógica de la exclusión', p. 33.

155 Isabel Rauber, *Profetas del cambio* (Havana: MEPLA, 1997), p. 27.

156 Alfonso Coñoecar, 'Fortalecer la organización popular', *América Libre*, 10 (special issue, January 1997), pp. 145–7.

157 *Ibid.*, p. 146.

158 Cited in Isabel Rauber, *Profetas del cambio*, p. 72.

159 F. Hinkelammert, 'La lógica de la exclusión', p. 153.

160 Adolfo SánchezVázquez, 'Reexamen de la idea del socialismo', paper given at the Round Table 85 at the International Forum 'Socialism in the World',Yugoslavia, October 1985, in *Escritos de política y filosofía* (Madrid: Ed. Ayuso y Fundación de Estudios marxistas, 1987), p.155.

161 Carlos Ruiz, 'La centralidad de la política en la acción revolucionaria' (mimeographed document, Santiago de Chile, 1998), p.13.

162 Helio Gallardo, 'Elementos para una discusión sobre la izquierda política en América Latina', *Pasos*, 50 (November–December 1993), p. 25.

163 David Hernández Castro, 'La revolución democrática (Otro mundo es posible)', document written for the Sixth Federal Assembly of the United Left, Molina de Segura (Murcia), 6 September 2000.

164 C. Ruiz, 'La centralidad de la política', p. 14.

165 *Ibid.*, p. 12.

166 *Ibid.*, p. 13.

167 *Ibid.*, p. 49.

168 Hardt and Negri, *Multitude* (note 28), p. 217.

169 Eric Hobsbawm, 'Identity Politics and the Left', *New Left Review* 217, May/June 1996.

170 Vladimir Lenin, 'The collapse of the Second International', in V. I. Lenin, *Collected Works*, Vol. 21 (Moscow: Progress Publishing House, 1964).

171 Conversation in Havana with Lito Marín and Nelson Gutiérrez, May 1989.
172 Noam Chomsky, *Necessary Illusions: Thought Control in Democratic Society* (London: Pluto Press, 1990) pp. vii.
173 Noam Chomsky, 'El control de los medios' (note 69), p. 14.
174 Benjamin Ginsberg, *The Captive Public* (Basic Books, 1986), pp. 86–9, quoted by Chomsky in *Necessary Illusions*, p. 7.
175 N. Chomsky, 'El Control de los medios' (note 69), p. 17.
176 Juan Antonio Blanco, *Tercer Milenio* (note 1), p. 58.
177 *Ibid.*, p. 62.
178 'During a revolution, millions and tens of millions of people learn in a week more than they do in a year of ordinary, somnolent life. For at the time of a sharp turn in the life of an entire people it becomes particularly clear what aims the various classes are pursuing, what strength they possess, and what methods they use.' 'Lessons of the Revolution', V. I. Lenin, *Collected Works*, Vol. 25 (Moscow: Progress Publishers, 1964), p. 227.
179 C. Ruiz, 'La centralidad de la política' (note 161), p. 15.
180 *Ibid.*
181 V. I. Lenin, 'The collapse of the Second International', (note 170), p. 251; M. Harnecker, *Vanguardia y crisis actual*, p. 87.
182 'Through circulation the common human species is composed, a multicolored Orpheus of infinite power....' Hardt and Negri, *Multitude* (note 28), p. 361.
183 Hardt and Negri, *Multitude* (note 28), p. 238.
184 *Ibid.*, p. 226.
185 *Ibid.*, p. 223.
186 *Ibid.*, p. 222.
187 *Ibid.*, p. 220.
188 Enrique Rubio, 'Perspectivas para el socialismo en el mundo actual', talk at the seminar 'Crisis y perspectivas del socialismo' organised by *Brecha* magazine, November 1991, mimeograph, p. 13.
189 C. Almeyda, 'Sobre la dimensión orgánica' (note 106), pp. 18–19.
190 Gutenberg was the inventor of typesetting, from which printing in Europe developed.
191 Atilio Borón, 'El fracaso y el triunfo del neoliberalismo', *América Libre*, No 10 (special edition), Buenos Aires, 1997, p. 17.
192 Marta Harnecker, 'Movimiento de los Trabajadores Rurales Sin Tierra: construyendo fuerza social antineoliberal', *Surda*, 23 (Santiago de Chile (November–December 1999).
193 C. Almeyda, 'Cambiar también la organización partidaria', *Convergencia*, 19–20 (February–March 1991), p. 37.
194 Carlos Ruiz, 'La centralidad de la política en la acción revolucionaria', unpublished document, Santiago de Chile, 1998, p. 13.
195 Adolfo Gilly, 'América Latina abajo y afuera', paper presented at the Second Winter Symposium on 'Las Américas en el horizonte del cambio'.
196 On this point see the resolutions passed by the Partido de los Trabajadores de Brasil (Brazilian Workers' Party) at its first Congress in 1991 (27 November–1 December) in *Resoluçoes do 1º Congresso do PT* (Resolutions of the First PT Congress).
197 H. Gallardo, 'Elementos para una discusión sobre la izquierda política en América Latina', *Pasos*, 50, November–December 1993, p. 29.
198 *Ibid.*, p. 31.
199 Enrique Rubio and Marcelo Pereira, *Utopía y estrategia, democracia y socialismo* (Monte-

video: Ed. Trilce, Uruguay, 1994), p. 151.

200 Helio Gallardo, 'Globalización neoliberal y alternativas populares', *Surda* 12 (June 1997), p. 13.

201 *Ibid.*

202 A. Sánchez Vázquez, 'Democracia, revolución y socialismo', *Travesía*, 1 (Peru, March 1991), p. 64.

203 Jon Elster, *An Introduction to Karl Marx* (Mexico City: Siglo XXI, 1992), p. 172.

204 In the original there is an untranslatable play on words 'no hay que confundir "estado de derecho" [the rule of law] con "estado de derecha" [right-wing state]'.

205 Adolfo Sánchez Vázquez, *Democracia, revolución*, p. 62.

206 *Ibid.*

207 Octavio Alberola, 'Etica y revolución', *El Viejo Topo*, 19 (Madrid, April 1978), 35.

208 O. Núñez, *La insurrección de la conciencia* (Managua: Escuela de Sociología de la Universidad Centroamericana, 1988), p. 29.

209 *Ibid.*, p. 60.

210 Ernesto Guevara, 'Socialism and Man in Cuba', in *Che, Selected Works of Ernesto Guevara* (Cambridge: MIT Press, 1969), p. 158.

211 O. Nuñez, *La Insurrección*, p. 272.

212 E. Guevara, 'Socialism and Man', p. 169.

213 On the subject of double standards in Cuba, see the excellent work of Fernando González, Dario Machado, Juan Luis Martín, and Emilio Sánchez, 'Notas para un debate acerca del hombre nuevo', keynote paper at the Seminar, Socialismo y el Hombre en Cuba, Havana, Cuba, 1988, pp. 31–56.

214 C. Almeyda, 'Sobre la dimensión orgánica' (note 106), p. 18.

215 C. Almeyda, 'Cambio social y concepto de partido', (1994) mimeo, p. 4.

216 C. Almeyda, Sobre la dimensión orgánica' (note 106), p. 17.

217 C. Almeyda, 'Cambiar también la organización partidaria' (note 193), pp. 35–6.

218 Ernesto Guevara, 'Socialism and Man', p. 158.

219 Orlando Núñez, 'La Insurreción' (note 28), p. 20.

220 *Ibid.*, p. 144.

221 Fernando González, Darío Machado, Juan Luis Martín, and Emilio Sánchez, 'Notas para un debate acerca' (note 213), p. 48.

222 This characteristic of being an activist is extraordinarily well reflected in the biography of Tina Modotti, who was romantically involved with Julio Antonio Mella for a while. Elena Poniatowska, *Tinísima* (Harmondsworth: Penguin Books, 1998).

223 E. Guevara, 'Socialism and Man in Cuba' (note 210), p. 168.

224 H. Gallardo, 'Elementos para una discusión sobre la izquerida política en América Latina', *Pasos,* 50 (November–December 1993), p. 26.

225 M. Harnecker, *Vanguardia y crisis actual* (note 123), pp. 63–9; 79.

226 I. Wallerstein, *After Liberalism* (New York: The New Press, 1995), pp. 249–50. This quote is from his article, 'The Collapse of Liberalism', also published in *Socialist Register* (London: Merlin Press, 1992).

227 M. Harnecker, *Vanguardia y crisis actual* (note 123), pp. 69–71.

228 Tarso Genro, quoted by Marta Harnecker in *Aprendiendo a gobernar (Alcaldía de Porto Alegre)* (Caracas: MEPLA-Alcaldía de Caracas, 1993), p. 14.

229 M. Harnecker, *Vanguardia y crisis actual* (note 123), pp. 64–7.

230 T. Genro, 'Seminario sobre el modo petista de gobernar', mimeograph, 1996.

231   *Ibid.*

232   C. Almeyda, *Cambiar también la organización partidaria* (note 193), p. 36; Enrique Rubio, 'Perspectivas para el socialismo' (note 188), p. 13.

233   E. Rubio, 'Perspectivas para el socialismo', p. 12.

234   M. Harnecker, *Vanguardia y crisis actual* (note 123), pp. 30–3.

235   One of the early members of *New Left Review* and one of the best-known contemporary European Marxists, a friend of Cuba and supporter of Latin American revolutionary processes.

236   Perry Anderson. 'The Antinomies of Antonio Gramsci', *New Left Review*, No.100, 1976, pp. 43–4.

237   A. Gramsci, *Maquiavelo y Lenin* (Santiago de Chile: Ed. Popular Nacimiento, 1971), pp.76–7.

238   E. Rubio and M. Pereira, *Utopía y estrategia* (note 199), p. 149.

239   M. Harnecker, *Intendencia de Montevideo: Un pueblo que se constituye en gobierno* (Caracas: Ed. MEPLA–Alcaldía de Caracas-Dirección de Cultura de la Gobernación del Estado de Bolívar, 1995).

240   M. Harnecker, *De armonías y conflictos (Alcaldías de Santos y Diadema)* (Caracas: Ed. MEPLA-Alcaldía de Caracas (Dirección de Imprenta Municipal), 1993), Venezuela; *Aprendiendo a gobernar (Alcaldía de Porto Alegre)* (Caracas: Ed. MEPLA-Alcaldía de Caracas (Dirección de Imprenta Municipal), 1993); *Triturados por el aparato institucional (Alcaldía de Vitoria)* (Caracas: Ed. MEPLA-Alcaldía de Caracas (Dirección de Imprenta Municipal), 1993); *Una alcaldía asediada (Alcaldía de Sao Paulo)*, (Caracas: Ed. MEPLA-Alcaldía de Caracas (Dirección de Imprenta Municipal), 1993).

241   M. Harnecker, *Caracas: La alcaldía donde se juega la esperanza* (Caracas: Ed. MEPLA-Fundarte-Instituto Municipal de Publicaciones (Alcaldía de Caracas), 1995); *Gobernar: tarea de todos (Alcaldía de Caroní)* (Caracas: MEPLA-Fundarte-Dirección de Imprenta Municipal, 1994).

242   For example, people say that the Brazilian PT (Workers Party) governments have a PT 'look'.

243   I describe it as such because it is a political organisation without formal membership, by-laws or programme, but one that came to have great influence in the union movement and in the impoverished neighbourhoods of Caracas.

244   See M. Harnecker, *Haciendo Camino al andar* (note 41), pp. 39–68.

245   *Ibid.*, pp. 67–117.

246   *Ibid.*, pp. 119–98.

247   The term 'public servant' is used in Brazil. I think it's a very appropriate term to refer to workers who provide public services.

248   M. Harnecker, *Haciendo camino al andar*, p. 15.

249   See M. Harnecker, *Sao Paulo, Una alcaldía asediada* (Caracas: Mepla, Cuba y Dirección de Imprenta Municipal, 1995), pp. 89–90.

250   See M. Harnecker, *Haciendo Camino al andar* (note 41), pp. 199–239.

251   Politicise does not mean partyise.

252   Cited in M. Harnecker, *Caracas, la alcaldía donde se juega la esperanza* (note 241), p. 17.

253   In Caracas it was called discussion of the *situado parroquial* (part of the budget devoted to each parish).

254   On this, see Marta Harnecker, *Delegando poder en la gente* (Havana: MEPLA, 1999); Caracas: Monte Ávila editores, 2004.

255 C. Vilas, 'La izquierda en América latina' (note 70), p. 52.
256 V. I. Lenin, 'The Importance of Gold Now and After Socialism's Total Victory', *Complete Works*, Vol. 35, p. 555. Marta Harnecker's emphasis.
257 Norberto Bobbio, *Diccionario de política* (México Siglo XXI, 1982), p. 1404.
258 V. I. Lenin, 'Two Roads', *Complete Works*, vol. 21, p. 219.
259 Rosa Luxemburg, *Reform or Revolution* (New York: Pathfinder Press, 1973), pp. 50–1.
260 C. Vilas, 'La izquierda en América Latina: presente y futuro' (note 70), p. 47.
261 *Ibid.*, p. 33.
262 H. Cores, quoted in Marta Harnecker, *Frente Amplio, Los desafíos de la izquierda legal* (Montevideo: Ediciones La República, 1991), p. 85.
263 C. Vilas, 'La izquierda en América Latina: presente', p. 46.
264 *Ibid.*, p. 34.
265 E. Rubio, 'Problemas de la lucha institucional en América Latina', in *América Libre*, 10 (special edition) (Buenos Aires: Argentina, January 1997), p. 118.
266 Luis Inácio da Silva, Brazilian union leader who rose to be the top leader of the Workers Party and then president of Brazil.
267 I am referring to Massimo Gorla, president of the parliamentary group Democrazia Proletaria, which stuck this label on the Italian Communist Party in an interview given to Miguel Barroso Ayats in *El Viejo Topo*, 1001 (June 1977), p. 42.
268 C. Vilas, 'La izquierda en América Latina', p. 54.
269 T. Genro, 'Seminario sobre el modo petista de gobernar' (note 230).
270 Miguel Barroso Ayats,' La izquierda en el parlamiento', (interview with Massimo Gorla) in 'Parlamentarismo y/o revolución', in the journal *El Viejo Topo*, No. 9, June 1977, Madrid pp.41–2.
271 In a speech by Hugo Chavéz at a forum organised by the newspapers *The National* and *Athenian of Caracas* on the Constitution, 23 September 1998.
272 The new Constitution of the Bolivarian Republic of Venezuela, Chapter IV: Political Rights and Popular Referendum, first section, on political rights. *Official Gazette* 30 December 1999, Caracas, Venezuela.
273 In Venezuela the municipalities are divided into parishes.
274 Dario L. Machados Rodríguez, 'La teoría del socialismo: más problemas que soluciones?' Paper given at the Karl Marx and the Challenges of the Twenty First Century conference in Havana, May 2006.
275 Marta Harnecker, *Los desafíos de la cogestión (Las experiencias de Cadafe y Cadela)* (Caracas: La Burbuja Editorial, April 2005).
276 Round-table meeting that took place on 26 February 2006, a transcript of which has not yet been published.
277 Michael Lebowitz, *Build It Now: Socialism for the Twenty-First Century* (New York: Monthly Review Press, 2006).

Index